FASHION KNITWEAR
DESIGN

FASHION KNITWEAR DESIGN

Edited by

Amy Twigger Holroyd and Helen Hill

THE CROWOOD PRESS

First published in 2019 by
The Crowood Press Ltd
Ramsbury, Marlborough
Wiltshire SN8 2HR

www.crowood.com

British Library Cataloguing-in-Publication Data
A catalogue record for this book is available from the British Library.

ISBN 978 1 78500 569 5

Frontispiece: Knitwear is a huge part of contemporary fashion, equally at home
on the catwalk and within our wardrobes.
DESIGNER: VERITY MILLER. PHOTOGRAPHER: DAVID BAIRD FOR NOTTINGHAM TRENT UNIVERSITY

Front cover: DESIGNER: JACARANDA BRAIN. PHOTOGRAPHERS: EMILY DRINKELD/HAO FU
Back cover, left: DESIGNER: KATE BAILEY. PHOTOGRAPHER: SOPHIE DIONNE PYKE
Back cover, right: PHOTOGRAPHER: RASHA KOTAICHE

Typeset by Peggy & Co. Design Inc.
Printed and bound in Printed and bound in India by Parksons Graphics

CONTENTS

INTRODUCTION

by Amy Twigger Holroyd

Take a look at what you are wearing today. Would you believe me if I told you that much of your outfit is knitted? There are, of course, the quintessential knitwear items: sweaters, cardigans, socks. But what about your underwear, your T-shirt, your sportswear? Although it might not be immediately obvious, the fabrics used for these items are also knitted. They share the same basic structure as that of a hand-knitted sweater, though they are produced on sophisticated industrial machines and at a much smaller scale. You might even be wearing knitted shoes: a recent innovation that exploits the knitted structure's unique capacity for three-dimensional shaping. Knitwear, then, is a huge part of contemporary fashion. What may initially seem to be a rather obscure specialism is actually a huge global industry, generating the garments that populate every rail, shelf and drawer of our wardrobes.

In terms of design, knitwear is a challenging and distinctive discipline, which blends the skills of the fashion designer with those of the textile designer. When we create knitwear, we design fabric and garment in one. Silhouette, texture, colour,

pattern, construction, detailing: all are under the creative control of the designer. Exploring these various dimensions of design provides ample scope for the creation of innovative fashion outcomes, whether flamboyant catwalk statements in eye-popping colour combinations or understated and elegant garments that are intended to be worn for a lifetime.

The knitted structure that we manipulate to produce our designs has unique characteristics in terms of stretch and shaping. These qualities are perhaps most apparent in the case of seamless knitwear: three-dimensional garments formed through the process of knitting, without the need for conventional seams. But they are also exploited in garments made by using the more familiar construction processes of fully fashioned knitwear, in which garment panels are knitted to shape, and cut-and-sew production, in which pieces are cut from knitted fabric.

Whatever the case, the knitwear designer is working with a simple yet amazingly versatile structure, with endless possibilities for creative exploration. Knitted fabrics can have highly diverse visual, physical and tactile properties. They can be produced by using centuries-old craft techniques or state-of-the-art digital technologies. They provide the opportunity to connect with culturally significant traditions, even while pushing technical boundaries. The discipline, therefore, offers incredible scope for experimentation and the development of a unique approach to design.

Knitting offers endless possibilities for design. This fabric, with three-dimensional qualities, knitted in organic cotton by designer Yena Moon, was created through the simple yet ingenious placement of knit and purl stitches.

Fig. 0.1 With this outfit, designer Kate Bailey has elegantly integrated metal components into a fine-gauge knitted fabric, challenging established perceptions of knitwear. PHOTOGRAPHER: SOPHIE DIONNE PYKE

Fig. 0.2 A classic men's knitwear shape can be reinvented for a contemporary fashion context through the inclusion of intricate integral patterning. DESIGNER: HELEN KAYE. PHOTOGRAPHER: JAMIE GORDON

Making the most of these possibilities demands a combination of creative insight and technical knowledge; the two are intertwined. In fact, researchers at the Open University who studied knitwear designers at work found that technical constraints had to be considered from the earliest stages of the design process. Another study found that knitwear design shares characteristics with both fashion design and engineering. Just like the fashion designer, the knitwear designer must be able to develop an original creative concept, generate garment ideas and resolve these ideas into workable designs by using their own in-depth understanding of the industry, the wearer and emerging trends. But, like the engineer, they must initiate and shape their ideas by using a deep awareness of how the designs might be produced, bearing in mind the distinctive

capacities and limitations of the knitted structure. It is no wonder that the skills of the knitwear designer are in high demand.

About the book

This book has been written by the team of specialists who deliver Nottingham Trent University's undergraduate and postgraduate courses in fashion knitwear design. BA (Hons) Fashion Knitwear Design and Knitted Textiles is the only undergraduate course delivered within the UK to focus solely on fashion knitwear design, while the MA in Fashion Knitwear Design supports students to further develop their creative and technical expertise. With decades of experience in teaching

Fig. 0.3 The vast majority of knitwear is produced in a factory environment, such as that of the Jack Masters industrial knitting plant in Leicester.
COURTESY: JACK MASTERS LTD

fashion knitwear design, the university has an international reputation for excellence and an impressive roll call of alumni working internationally in all areas of the industry.

The nine authors have extensive and varied experience of professional knitwear design, encompassing design studios, manufacturing environments and trend-forecasting agencies; mass-market companies, designer labels and micro-scale businesses; and groundbreaking academic research. We have designed a diverse range of outcomes including knitted fabric swatches, knitwear collections, one-off items, shoes and non-wearable art pieces and have specialist interests including archives, sustainable design and innovative computer-aided design and manufacturing (CAD/CAM).

This expertise is captured within the eight chapters of the book, which take in the entire knitwear design process, along with the history of the industry and potential career routes. While each author has written about an area of particular interest, there are many threads that run across the book as a whole, and the content has been developed through discussion and collaborative reflection. As we have written the book, we have adopted an inclusive approach that covers a range of contexts, from micro-scale businesses to mass production and from student projects to professional practice. Whatever your place within the industry, you will benefit from a well-developed understanding of the way in which the industry operates and the diverse processes involved in taking a knitwear design from initial idea to finished product.

Fig. 0.4 Alternative contexts for knitwear production include small studios, where domestic and hand-flat knitting machines are often used.

Chapter by chapter

Chapter 1, by Cathy Challender, explores the history of knitting and knitwear, providing an overview of the developments that have led to today's dynamic industry. It explores the early beginnings of the craft, from medieval hand knitting to the invention of the stocking frame and the technological innovations that transformed the possibilities of knitting during the Industrial Revolution. The major shifts in knitwear styles and production contexts that occurred throughout the twentieth century and into the current era are discussed, along with a history of knitting as a hobby activity.

Chapter 2, by Claire Preskey, focuses on the research that drives any design project. Starting with a discussion of the design brief that kick-starts the process, it then explores key avenues of research. Market research involves studying existing ranges, brand identities and consumer profiles, while trend research requires the designer to pick up on emerging cultural shifts. The designer also needs to gather personal inspiration to develop a unique concept from which to design. The chapter concludes with advice on how to communicate this research in a professional manner.

Chapter 3, by Kandy Diamond, provides an introduction to the knitwear designer's raw material: yarn. It explores various natural, synthetic and regenerated fibres, explaining the link between their characteristics at a microscopic level and the properties of the knitwear that they are used to produce. The processes involved in turning these fibres into yarn are outlined, while a user-friendly guide demystifies yarn counts and types. The final section provides guidance to the designer on how to select yarns, weighing up a range of aesthetic, technological and practical factors.

Chapter 4, by Will Hurley, supports the designer to develop their knowledge of knitted structures and the technologies that are used to produce them. The key principles of weft and warp knitting are discussed, and an outline of the diverse range of knitting machines in use today is presented. An introduction to the basics of weft-knitted structures is followed by profiles of various single- and double-jersey fabrics, considering both the construction and the application of these fabrics in fashion contexts. To conclude, the chapter discusses the translation of designs by using digital industrial technologies.

Chapter 5, by Jane Thomson, investigates the development and communication of original knitwear designs. Picking up from Chapter 3, it discusses ways of responding to the material gathered during the research process in order to generate design ideas. Two sections then explore the central creative process of the knitwear designer: developing these ideas into coherent collections of knitted fabrics and knitted garments through drawing, sampling and working in three dimensions. A final section focuses on the communication of designs via fashion illustrations, garment flats and design boards.

Chapter 6, by Juliana Sissons, guides the designer through the process of creating a three-dimensional knitwear silhouette by using a range of approaches to pattern cutting. It describes the steps involved in flat-pattern cutting, creating and adapting basic blocks to generate two-dimensional pattern pieces. It then explains how to generate instructions, to guide the knitting of these pieces, including the calculation of the shapings required for fully fashioned construction. Alternative approaches to silhouette creation are discussed, including draping jersey or knitted samples on a mannequin, and geometric pattern cutting methods.

Chapter 7, by Helen Hill, completes the journey from design brief to finished garment, by outlining key aspects of knitwear construction. It starts by describing the different methods of manufacturing knitted garments, the machinery that is used

Fig. 0.6   This highly engineered jacquard fabric was created by Studio Eva x Carola, working in collaboration with circular-knitting-machine manufacturer Santoni to create innovative seamless textiles.

Fig. 0.5   The effective designer has a well-developed understanding of both the technical dimensions and the creative potential of knitting. Within this fabric collection, designer Charlotte Cameron has used a range of structures, including mock rib, bird's-eye jacquard cardigan, plating and all-needle rib.

and the global locations in which this manufacturing activity takes place. It then explains the stages of construction in detail, including instructions for the specialist process of linking. Focusing on the industrial context, the processes involved in preparing a design for production, including sampling and costing, are discussed. Finally, quality control, labelling, and care and repair are explored.

Chapter 8, by Ian McInnes, examines careers within the fashion knitwear industry. It discusses opportunities to design for established high street retailers and luxury brands, whether in-house or via suppliers. More independent roles are then considered, such as swatch design, freelance work, creating a fashion label and designing hand-knitting patterns. Finally, the alternative routes of trend forecasting, teaching and academic research are profiled. Case studies in every career-focused section provide valuable snapshots of the roles and responsibilities of specialists who have established themselves in various areas of the industry.

Looking forward

While the book offers vital insights into the practices of today's fashion knitwear industry, it is important to note that this is a world in flux. The fashion and textiles industry, of which knitwear is a part, is slowly facing up to its responsibilities in terms of global challenges such as climate change. The environmental and social problems associated with the production of clothes are significant and well documented, with negative impacts occurring in all phases of a garment's life cycle, from fibre production through to disposal. These problems have been exacerbated by the advent of fast fashion, which has brought about massive increases in the volume of garments produced, sold and prematurely discarded. Fashion is now widely acknowledged to be one of the most harmful industries in the world.

In response to these issues, brands and retailers are increasingly seeking to produce their knitwear in a more sustainable way, with consideration for energy use, pollution control and workers' rights. Indeed, the responsible sourcing of materials and selection of production methods should be an important aspect of every designer's work, and design strategies that aim to reduce waste and to slow consumption have great value. Some of these approaches are discussed in the chapters of this book. Yet these changes cannot, on their own, do any more than make a bad situation a little less bad; much more fundamental change is needed if we are to address the impact that our industry has on the planet and its people. In truth,

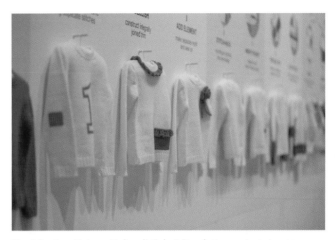

Fig. 0.7 Amy Twigger Holroyd's Reknit Revolution project aims to support home knitters to rework the knitted items in their wardrobes. In pursuing this project, Amy has shifted her design practice from creating collections of knitwear to developing resources that encourage others to act. PHOTOGRAPHER: JAMIE GREY AT RUGBY ART GALLERY & MUSEUM

we must question everything about the way that we produce, distribute, acquire, use, care for and dispose of our clothes.

To some, change may seem unthinkable; the established system appears entirely entrenched. However, as the historical perspective offered in Chapter 1 helps us to appreciate, the knitwear industry is not static; for centuries it has evolved, being shaped by economic, social and political forces and the potential of new technologies. These shifts will continue. In fact, as trend forecaster Helen Palmer explains in her case study in Chapter 8, 'the fashion and textiles industry is due for a disruptive and radical transformation'.

As future professionals within the industry, the students and young designers whom we have imagined as the readers of this book will be at the forefront of this transformation. This prospect may seem scary. Perhaps it is frustrating to get to grips with the workings of a complex industry, only to be told that it is about to change. But the skills that you develop as a knitwear designer should stand you in good stead to navigate, and even lead, this process of change. The deep understanding of materials, technologies and construction that is developed through the knitwear specialism will always be needed, even if not in quite the same way as today. The questioning approach that is inherent in the practice of design is of great value in imagining how things might be done differently. And the cultural awareness that enables designers to anticipate and even steer tastes and trends will support your ability to see opportunities for change. In short, these uncertain times require creative imagination and technical understanding – core skills of the fashion knitwear designer.

<table>
<tr><td>F</td><td>1</td><td>R</td><td>1</td></tr>
<tr><td>0</td><td>1</td><td>0</td><td>1</td></tr>
<tr><td>F</td><td>1</td><td>R</td><td>1</td></tr>
<tr><td>0</td><td>1</td><td>0</td><td>1</td></tr>
<tr><td>F</td><td>1</td><td>D</td><td>1</td></tr>
<tr><td>0</td><td>1</td><td>0</td><td>1</td></tr>
<tr><td>R</td><td>1</td><td>F</td><td>1</td></tr>
<tr><td>R</td><td>1</td><td>F</td><td>1</td></tr>
<tr><td>0</td><td>1</td><td>0</td><td>1</td></tr>
<tr><td>D</td><td>1</td><td>F</td><td>1</td></tr>
<tr><td>0</td><td>1</td><td>0</td><td>1</td></tr>
<tr><td>D</td><td>1</td><td>F</td><td>1</td></tr>
<tr><td>0</td><td>1</td><td>0</td><td>1</td></tr>
</table>

2/3 Sett Silk
15/8 Oeam
90 yeds of Silk
No 100 yeds Cotton
17 yeds Stiffness
150 Lisles Bottom & 75
D Spun

<table>
<tr><td>F</td><td>1</td><td>R</td><td>1</td></tr>
<tr><td>F</td><td>1</td><td>R</td><td>1</td></tr>
<tr><td>0</td><td>1</td><td>0</td><td>1</td></tr>
<tr><td>F</td><td>1</td><td>D</td><td>1</td></tr>
<tr><td>0</td><td>1</td><td>0</td><td>1</td></tr>
<tr><td>F</td><td>1</td><td>R</td><td>1</td></tr>
<tr><td>R</td><td>1</td><td>F</td><td>1</td></tr>
<tr><td>R</td><td>1</td><td>F</td><td>1</td></tr>
<tr><td>0</td><td>1</td><td>0</td><td>1</td></tr>
<tr><td>R</td><td>1</td><td>F</td><td>1</td></tr>
<tr><td>0</td><td>1</td><td>0</td><td>1</td></tr>
<tr><td>R</td><td>1</td><td>F</td><td>1</td><td>75</td><td>D S</td></tr>
</table>

<table>
<tr><td>F</td><td>1</td><td>0</td><td>1</td><td>0</td><td>1</td></tr>
<tr><td>0</td><td>1</td><td>0</td><td>1</td><td>F</td><td>1</td></tr>
<tr><td>0</td><td>1</td><td>0</td><td>1</td><td>R</td><td>2</td></tr>
<tr><td>F</td><td>1</td><td>R</td><td>3</td><td>R</td><td>2</td></tr>
<tr><td>R</td><td>1</td><td>0</td><td>1</td><td>0</td><td>1</td></tr>
<tr><td>R</td><td>1</td><td>0</td><td>1</td><td>0</td><td>1</td></tr>
<tr><td>0</td><td>1</td><td>0</td><td>1</td><td>R</td><td>1</td></tr>
<tr><td>0</td><td>1</td><td>0</td><td>1</td><td>R</td><td>1</td></tr>
<tr><td>R</td><td>1</td><td>F</td><td>3</td><td>F</td><td>2</td></tr>
</table>

No 170 Bottom 100 yeds
No 60 Spun 60 yeds mi
No 170 Liles & 15 Silk Twis
95 yeds Top Bean
28 guage 27 yeds Stiffn
26 guage 24 " Isle "
Bottom 120
Top 100 Twister

CHAPTER 1

HISTORY AND CONTEXT

by Cathy Challender

Introduction

In order to fully appreciate the context in which fashion knitwear is designed, manufactured, sold and worn today, it is important to gain an understanding of the history of the industry. The role of the fashion knitwear designer, the range of technologies used to produce knitted garments, the traditional styles that are referenced time after time: all can be traced back through centuries of expertise and innovation.

This chapter provides an overview of the development of knitting and knitwear, from a medieval craft to contemporary practices, via the seismic shifts of the Industrial Revolution. It explores technological developments, from the stocking frame to today's machines capable of seamless knitting, and outlines the different strands of the industry that have been created along the way. We will consider the changes in fashion that drove these technological changes, the iconic styles that have emerged and the influential designers who have pushed the boundaries of fashion knitwear over the years. The chapter concludes with an examination of hobby knitting, tracking hand knitting from a respectable Victorian pastime through to a newly reinvigorated twenty-first-century leisure pursuit.

This page from a ledger dated 1859 presents silk warp-knitted samples and manufacturing notes. It is thought to have belonged to Ball and Co., a warp-knitting manufacturer operating in Ilkeston and Nottingham.

The early industry

Although hand knitting is now primarily known as a hobby activity, it was once a common source of income across Britain and beyond. The practice gradually disappeared with the introduction of the knitting frame, which dramatically speeded up production. This first machine, invented in 1589 to produce fashionable stockings, laid the foundations for today's technology.

Hand knitting

While the origins of hand knitting are not known, it is certain that the craft is relatively recent in comparison to weaving, which is believed to date back to Palaeolithic times. The earliest examples of hand knitting are fragments of a stocking, discovered in Egypt, dating from the tenth century AD, that display evidence of knitting being a well-established technique. Although we can only speculate about the development of knitting up to this point, earlier archaeological finds provide clues about potential influences. Socks, mittens and head coverings made by using nalbinding – a technique that produces a sturdy fabric that resembles knitting but is made in a different way, by using short lengths of yarn and one flat needle – date from the fourth or fifth century AD onwards.

Fig. 1.1 This pair of woollen socks, made in Egypt in the fourth or fifth century, was constructed by using nalbinding, a knotless netting technique that predates true knitting. © VICTORIA AND ALBERT MUSEUM

Fig. 1.2 During medieval and Renaissance times, the knitting of woollen caps, such as those illustrated, was an important industry in Britain. The process of capping involved the knitting and felting (fulling) of caps to make them weatherproof; they were then shorn, to give a smooth appearance to the fabric.

While the Egyptian stocking proves that knitting would have been practised during medieval times, further evidence is frustratingly scarce. Most agree that knitting originated in the Middle East, spreading via trade and colonization to Europe and the Americas. Requiring no heavy equipment, the craft was easily portable. The types of articles made through knitting at this time would have been diverse, but understandably it is the most precious items, such as liturgical gloves, that have survived. A series of paintings known as *Knitting Madonna*, from the fourteenth century, show garments being knitted as a seamless tube on four needles, indicating the technique being used and suggesting an important and established industry.

The British seem to have taken readily to hand knitting. The established woollen industry supplied raw material, and the craft became an important source of income in the medieval period. British craftspeople gained a reputation for supplying superior-quality woollen caps and then stockings to Europe and the American colonies. The first knitting guilds were founded in Europe during the thirteenth century, growing in importance during the sixteenth century. These powerful organizations controlled the trade, enforcing standards and rules. The master knitters of the guilds were an elite who travelled, became educated in foreign knitting techniques and were closely allied to the fullers and wool merchants. Qualification as a master required the production of a cap, stockings, a vest and finally a highly complex patterned blanket. When the demand for knitted caps waned, several acts of parliament were passed to protect the knitters' interests; one enforced the wearing of a woollen knitted cap on Sundays and holidays. Known as The Statute of Servants because the rich were exempt from adhering to it, the act was unpopular and had only limited success.

During the sixteenth century, an emerging men's fashion for very short breeches placed an emphasis on the leg. Stockings had previously been made of woven cloth; the elastic properties of hand-knitted stockings made them much more suitable for wear. Paintings from the period show the prominence of the stocking in the royal court, particularly for men. Stockings became increasingly splendid for those who could afford them, with the finest examples being imported at great cost from Spain or Italy. Less is known about women's stockings at this time; propriety forbade even the mention of women's legs or the stockings that women wore. Similarly, little is known about the highly refined silk and wool undershirts that were produced during the seventeenth century. A rare exception is a gory account of the knitted shirt supposedly worn by King Charles I at his execution in 1649. This 'ghastly relic' was described as a shirt of great perfection, no doubt the work of a master knitter.

The elite knitters were a minority, located in the European textiles centres or close to the royal courts. In most regions, the craft was practised as a necessary part-time supplement to other forms of income such as farming or fishing. Hand knitting was encouraged to allow the rural poor to be self-sufficient; to facilitate this, a number of knitting schools had been established in England and continental Europe as early as the sixteenth century. Yet, in reality, knitting provided only a meagre existence for the vast majority of knitters. By the eighteenth century, when stockings produced more quickly and cheaply by machine had begun to overtake the market, hand knitting remained in rural or coastal areas only, where knitting could still supplement incomes from crofting or fishing. The production of Guernsey frocks, a type of working garment adopted by sailors and fishermen from the nineteenth century onwards, provided work for hand knitters. Although the regional patterns for a fisherman's sturdy, hand-knitted gansey could be elaborate, the knitting of ganseys was not a lucrative activity. The

Fig. 1.3 A portrait of Richard Sackville, Earl of Dorset, painted by William Larkin in 1613. Sackville, known for his lavish lifestyle and extravagant wardrobe, is depicted wearing hand-knitted silk stockings that are embellished at the ankles.

Fig. 1.4 This representation of a spring bearded needle from a Lee stocking frame (hand frame) depicts the needle's three important parts: the shank upon which the old loop was formed; the beard, which retains the new loop and enables the old one to pass off; and the eye, which receives the end of the beard.

decline continued; by the middle of the nineteenth century, with the notable exception of the knitting performed by the knitters of the Shetland Islands, hand knitting as an industry was permanently diminished.

The stocking frame

The stocking frame, or hand frame, regarded by many as one of the most important inventions of the Renaissance, was invented in 1589, when the fashion for knitted stockings was at its height. Its inventor, Reverend William Lee of Calverton in Nottinghamshire, had aimed to create a machine that would enable him to emulate a hand-knitted stocking. He combined the shape of the upright weaving loom with an entirely new way of making the loops that form a knitted fabric. This method used a row of 'bearded' needles arranged horizontally, with one end of each needle fixed into a needle bed; rather than each stitch being worked individually, as in hand knitting, all of the needles formed loops simultaneously. This technology dramatically speeded up the process of knitting, far beyond the capacity of even the swiftest hand knitter.

Lee's first stockings were made of wool, knitted at a relatively coarse gauge equivalent to today's 8 gauge knitting machines. Despite the inventive brilliance of the machine, Queen Elizabeth I denied Lee a patent because she felt that his invention would harm the livelihoods of British hand knitters. She indicated that, if Lee's machine could knit silk stockings to compete with foreign imports, his request would be viewed more favourably. With help from skilled French artisans, Lee achieved this task: by 1599, his frame could knit silk stockings and waistcoats. Still denied support from the English court, he relocated to Rouen, a centre for textiles in France. He hoped for more favourable treatment from King Henri IV, but these hopes were dashed when the king was assassinated. Lee died in France without seeing the full reward for his efforts.

The use of the stocking frame was, however, growing. While a growing number of frames were soon being used in the East Midlands and as far away as Dublin, for producing woollen stockings, the majority of frames were based in London, close to the royal court. Here, silk stockings and other items were made with an eye to the latest fashions – now with the fabric at a much finer gauge. Despite the success of the trade, it was not until 1657 that the Worshipful Company of Framework Knitters was incorporated by Oliver Cromwell. The company controlled the organization of the industry and the taking on

Fig. 1.5 The buildings that are now Ruddington Framework Knitters' Museum in Nottinghamshire were formerly frame-knitting workshops. The distinctive long windows maximized the light available for performing the highly skilled craft of framework knitting.

with the fashion of the day. Just a few years later, the Petinet knitting machine enabled ornamental pierced patterns to be automatically added into the 'clock' of a stocking, at the ankle. In a further significant development, the stocking frame was mechanized by Samuel Wise in 1769. These improvements, together with the appeal of the fine fabrics that could now be achieved by the machine, meant that, by the end of the eighteenth century, frame-knitted stockings were more popular than stockings that were produced by hand.

The Industrial Revolution

The deep societal and economic changes brought about by the Industrial Revolution in the eighteenth and nineteenth centuries transformed every aspect of British life – including, inevitably, the knitting industry. Technological innovations and a shift to factory production, coupled with changes in fashion, led to machines being used to produce a wider range of garments.

of apprentices; in the early days, it limited development with a succession of rules and regulations. In rural areas further from London, especially in the East Midlands, the company was less able to exert its influence. By the early eighteenth century, the use of the frame had progressed sufficiently for the towns and villages around Nottingham, Leicester and Derby to become a centre for stocking-making of all types.

The first frame-knitted stockings were knitted flat by machine and then seamed by hand; this was an important and distinctive feature. The calf and foot shapings were achieved through the manual removal of stitches from the selvedge needles, producing the same distinctive fashioning marks as achieved by hand knitting. However, the replication of hand-knitted stitches required laborious effort on the part of the framework knitter. The purl (reverse) stitches so easily formed by hand had to be made on the frame by individually laddering then reworking a stitch from the opposite direction. Rib fabrics, which combine columns of knit and purl stitches, are therefore particularly difficult to work on the early Lee frame.

A succession of technical developments during the eighteenth century enhanced the machine's capabilities. The invention of the tuck presser in 1740, for example, introduced the possibility of patterning on the frame. In 1758, Jedediah Strutt from Derby patented the rib attachment – a second set of needles added to Lee's stocking frame. The rib fabrics produced were more elastic, giving an improved fit that was in accordance

A changing stocking industry

Before the Industrial Revolution, it took up to five hand spinners to keep the stocking knitter supplied with yarn. In the second half of the eighteenth century, spinning was moving out of the home and into the efficient production-focused environment of the mills. This shift was prompted by a succession of inventions, including those of James Hargreaves' horse-powered spinning jenny in 1764, Richard Arkwright's water frame in 1771 and Samuel Crompton's spinning mule in 1779, which vastly increased yarn production. With yarn being readily available, it was the framework knitters – still working in the home – who were struggling to keep up with the demands of the industry.

Typically, men operated the knitting frames; this was an arduous and skilful task. It could take years to become a master knitter of fancy goods and earn enough to generate and sustain a sufficient income. Even then, framework knitting provided only a precarious livelihood. Women and children undertook preparation of the yarn; women also seamed the stockings. The specialist task of chevening (embroidering) women's stockings was undertaken by women and girls, who were usually poorly paid outworkers or apprentices, housed under the supervision of a mistress. Some successful framework knitters of this period – along with men from unrelated trades – set themselves up as hosiers, renting frames out to other knitters, to work at their own homes, and organizing the supply and distribution of

Fig. 1.6   G.H. Hurt & Son Ltd, manufacturers of fine lace shawls, was established in 1912 in Chilwell, Nottingham. Master knitter Mr Henry Hurt, the grandson of the company's founder, is one of the few people able to work an eighteenth-century hand frame today.
COURTESY: G.H. HURT & SON LTD

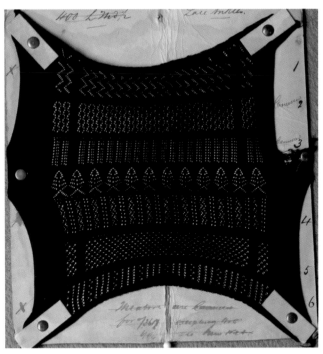

Fig. 1.7   This nineteenth-century framework-knitted sampler shows lace patterns for stockings, produced by Allen Solly & Co. Ltd of Nottingham. This influential family firm supplied many of the royal families of Europe.

yarn and finished goods. If the hosier had sufficient workshop floor space, he might employ knitters and keep apprentices to work a number of frames within the workshop. Some hosiers acquired considerable fortunes; this imbalance of power caused considerable friction between the individual knitter and the powerful hosier. The introduction of frame rents, which essentially passed on all of the costs of production to the knitter, exacerbated this situation and led to the outbreak of Luddite riots in Nottinghamshire.

Various influences, including wars with the French that resulted in short supplies and trade embargoes, led to a downturn in the industry in the early nineteenth century. A change in fashion had a significant impact: the introduction of trousers for men rendered full-length stockings unnecessary. The fashionable and upper classes abandoned breeches and stockings for full-length trousers and half hose (socks); a trend for knee-high boots meant that not a glimpse of hosiery could

be seen. Stockings could no longer command the high prices of preceding eras, and the inexorable decline of the stocking as a men's fashion item had begun.

Another shift in fashion, however, was to drive a new wave of technical innovation. Responding to the fashionableness of expensive handmade lace, inventors concentrated on developing the stocking frame to produce a viable substitute. The earliest piece of machine-made lace is credited to hosier Robert Frost. Along with other early developments, this innovation provided work to framework knitters and thousands of female embroiders who decorated the resultant fabric. John Heathcoat developed the technology further and in 1809 patented his bobbin-net machine, giving rise to the wealthy Nottingham lace industry of the nineteenth century. Men working the lace-making machines earned several times as much as a framework knitter.

Knitting innovations

While the British hosiery industry entered a period of stagnation during the nineteenth century, French, American and German inventors strove to increase the speed at which knitted fabrics

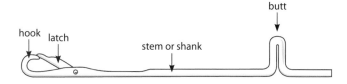

Fig. 1.8 The latch needle, invented in 1847, revolutionized knitting technology and is still in use in the latest machines. The latch enables a stitch to be formed as the needle slides forward and backward, picking up the yarn and drawing it through the loop of the stitch from the previous course.

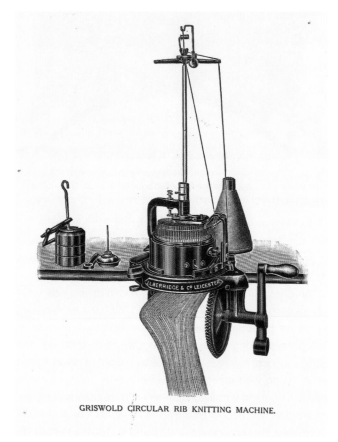

GRISWOLD CIRCULAR RIB KNITTING MACHINE.

Fig. 1.9 Dating from the late nineteenth century, the Griswold hand-cranked, circular sock-knitting machine was used both for production in workshops and by the home knitter. Circular sock-knitting machines were put into active service in both world wars, for the knitting of army socks.

could be produced. Their major innovations commenced with the invention of the circular frame in France in 1798. The needles of this machine were arranged in a rotating ring; this arrangement was well suited for conversion of the machine to be run by steam power. Although the British were slow to adopt this revolutionary machine, in America, it was further

developed in the mid-nineteenth century in order to meet the growing demand for mass-produced knitted goods. At this time, the circular knitting machine could produce an amazing 350 courses of knitted fabric a minute.

In 1847, the self-acting or latch needle was invented by Matthew Townsend of Leicester, improving upon the bearded needle used in the original frame. The impact of this small yet revolutionary invention can hardly be imagined. Townsend's needle was widely adopted by the circular-knitting-machine industry in the USA for its speed, versatility and simplicity of operation. And it was not just the large-scale circular knitting machines that utilized the new technology: small, circular, latch-needle machines such as the Griswold and the Harrison 'Little Rapid' were produced for domestic use. These machines were advertised in women's magazines, targeting those wanting to earn extra money by knitting socks and other items at home.

The invention of a series of patterning mechanisms enabled the knitting of patterns, textures and colour changes. Though initially and famously applied to the weaving loom by J.M. Jacquard in 1805, the punchcard patterning mechanism was applied to a wide range of knitting machines throughout the nineteenth century. Increasingly decorative novelty fabrics, affordable for the middle and lower end of the market, were produced. Another significant development was warp knitting. The first warp technology, invented in England during the eighteenth century, was an attachment for the hand frame and was used mainly to decorate stockings. In the nineteenth century, German manufacturers developed the potential of the warp attachment as a machine in its own right. Warp-knitted fabrics are ideal for items where more stability is required in the fabric and for cut goods such as gloves.

Transforming the frame

While knitters were still working the hand frame in their homes in the mid-nineteenth century, steam power and factory production were soon to transform the industry. Associated with a series of patents made starting in 1860, the Cotton's steam-powered frame brought together good ideas previously pioneered by other inventors. While this innovative 'straight-bar' machine still employed bearded needles and had many parts that were similar to those of the hand frame, it used a flatbed to produce fully fashioned garments, automatically shaped at the selvedges, for the first time. At the time, the Cotton's frame was considered to be the most important development since William Lee's invention of the very first frame. In comparison to

Fig. 1.10 Established in 1784, John Smedley Ltd is the world's oldest knitwear manufacturer. The entire production operation is carried out on their site at Lea Mills in Derbyshire. COURTESY: JOHN SMEDLEY LTD

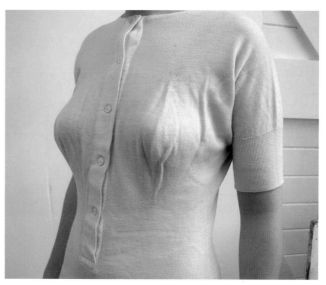

Fig. 1.11 Dating from the early twentieth century, a lady's fully fashioned woollen combination garment, featuring seamless breast gores. The complex shaping of the knitting conforms comfortably to the contours of the body, without any seaming at the bust: this is important when the garment is to be worn with a corset.

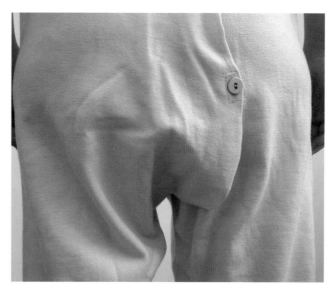

Fig. 1.12 A woollen combination garment, featuring a buttoned opening on the bottom.

its forerunners, this machine was a giant. Its size, coupled with the move to steam power, necessitated the move from domestic production into large purpose-built factories, transforming the skylines of Nottingham and Leicester.

The Cotton's frame had a major impact on manufacturing: first eight, then twelve and later up to thirty-six automatically narrowed stocking lengths could be produced at once. Furthermore, the number of men needed to operate the new machines steadily reduced. With the machine's gentle knitting action, fine wool yarns could be used for the first time. These factors made the Cotton's machine suitable for the increasingly important production of knitted underwear garments. While hand-frame knitters in the Scottish Borders had concentrated on making high-quality underwear for the home and export market since the 1830s, production using the Cotton's frame meant that quality knitted underwear was affordable for the middle classes for the first time. Demand steadily grew for these items, driven in no small part by German guru Dr Gustav Jaeger, who advocated the use of full-body, woollen, knitted undergarments, known as combinations, to promote health. His 'sanitary underwear' was produced by John Smedley Ltd in Derbyshire until the Jaeger factory and brand were established. Jaeger was ahead of his time and soon inspired other manufacturers who recognized that the elastic, health-promoting properties of knitwear could be exploited across a range of intimate items.

While some making-up, trimming and finishing of hosiery and underwear would continue in the home, much of this activity would soon join the working of the knitting frames in the factory setting. This shift was driven, once again, by the invention of new technology and the introduction of steam power. Linking machines (also called linkers), used to join knitted fabrics together with a chain stitch, were invented by a Nottingham company, B. Hague, and first installed in a factory in 1866. Julius Kohler invented the cup seamer in 1874 to quickly join the selvedges of shaped goods. Standard lock-stitch sewing machines were also used for attaching non-elastic trims.

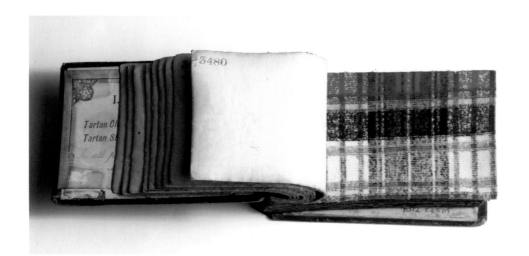

Fig. 1.13 This highly complex and labour-intensive framework-knitted intarsia fabric in Dress Stuart tartan pattern was produced by I.R. Morley. Supplying the royal court, the company thrived during the time of the domestic system and later expanded to a factory environment.
COURTESY: RUDDINGTON FRAMEWORK KNITTERS' MUSEUM

These processes required skill; it took months of practice before women, paid by the piece, could earn sufficient remuneration for their work.

By the end of the nineteenth century, new inventions were also being applied to the construction of knitwear made from circularly knitted fabric in the USA; these inventions would have a huge impact on the quality of mass-produced knitwear. The crochet machine, invented by The Merrow Machine Company in 1868, was developed into the industrial overlock machine and produced in large numbers by the 1890s, providing an affordable and reliable way of manufacturing cut-and-sew knitted underwear and removing the stigma that had previously been associated with such items.

Although the vast majority of knitting production had shifted to the factory system by the late nineteenth century, a small number of hand frames were still being used, supplying niche markets such as the knitted-lace-shawl trade. A few knitters were supported by work for the firms who supplied the royal court, where breeches and silk stockings were still worn. Companies including Elliot's of Swanwick, I.R. Morley and Allen Solly & Co. Ltd have had a long history of employing skilled craftsmen and women to make fine quality silk hosiery for royalty; their order books kept the old framework knitters in the villages occupied well into the twentieth century.

Flatbed machines

The machine most familiar to knitters today is the flatbed or V-bed machine, which was invented by American Isaac W. Lamb in 1863. Advertised as 'a home knitter machine: easy to handle and cheap as a sewing machine', this was the first machine to fully utilize the versatility of the latch needle. Lamb's hand-flat machine had two beds, each positioned at a 45-degree angle, for knitting ribs. In the past, needles had moved as a group; Lamb invented a device to lift and lower them individually one after another with great rapidity, increasing the design capabilities of the machine. He continued to develop the machine to allow the knitting of thirty different stitch patterns, paving the way for the flexible flatbed machines of today. The machines were taken up straight away, not only for the production of fashioned hosiery but also for production for the newly emerging sweater market. During the 1860s, a large number of Lamb's machines were employed in Leicester in the production of working men's cardigans.

Lamb sold the European rights to his invention to Edouard Dubied of Neuchâtel. The Dubied company continued to improve the machine throughout the nineteenth century, and the machine has proved to have enduring appeal: Dubied hand-flat machines are still used in small studios and design colleges, and even for production in some parts of the world. In 1881, Grosser obtained a patent for jacquard patterning. Hand flats with this function enabled the machine production of the patterned golf and other sporting sweaters that had become favoured by the upper classes during the nineteenth century.

By the early twentieth century, power could be applied to these machines, making them suitable for the commercial production of affordable knitted outerwear. In 1900, a revolutionary hand-flat machine, the Flatbed Split Purl knitting machine, was invented by Heinrich Stoll in Germany. Known as a links-links machine, the new invention used horizontal beds and double-ended needles to replicate the purl stitch of hand knitting that had evaded machine knitters for so long.

Into the twentieth century

The twentieth century saw knitted outerwear become increasingly popular, with the emergence of enduring styles that are still being produced today. Rapidly changing fashions, the development of new fibres, and advances in technology took knitwear into new applications in a process of ongoing evolution.

Underwear to outerwear

From the beginning of the twentieth century, knitted sweaters, jackets, waistcoats and cardigans were becoming everyday garments; in response, firms began to diversify production from underwear to outerwear. One of the influences for this shift was the increased opportunity for the middle and working classes to wear leisure clothes. A series of social reforms led to the provision of sporting facilities and shorter working hours to allow for recreation. Walking, cycling, golf and team sports, such as football, were now encouraged for all and required appropriate, affordable clothing. Thus, the sporting sweater crossed class boundaries and eventually influenced the take-up of the sweater as a fashion garment.

By the 1920s, the desire for comfortable knitted clothing had developed into a sweater craze: knitwear was at the forefront of fashion revolution. Diverse and flamboyant styles developed; for example, by using intarsia to turn sweaters into abstract pictures. While wool was still widely used, viscose – the first man-made fibre – became more common, and it was used with jacquard patterning to create fluid and lightweight art deco-style items. Coco Chanel notably recognized the fashion potential of knitted fabrics for outerwear. She repurposed overlooked fabrics such as jersey, a utility fabric previously used for underwear.

Fig. 1.14 Dubied hand-flat machines, developed in the nineteenth century, are still used today. They are excellent machines on which to learn the fundamentals of the knitting process.

One of the most iconic sweaters of the period was the hand-knitted *trompe l'œil* bow sweater, designed by Elsa Schiaparelli in 1927 and inspired by surrealist art. Meanwhile, Jean Patou, a designer and sports enthusiast, produced streamlined fine-gauge knitwear, which was taken up by the sun-loving leisured classes. Together, these influential designers introduced a style of knitwear that would remain a fashion staple throughout the twentieth century.

Along with knitted outerwear, the 1920s and 1930s saw the emergence of knitted swimwear for women. The first knitted swimming costumes for men had appeared in the 1870s, knitted on circular knitting machines and constructed in one piece, just like underwear, with a buttoned front. Considered too revealing, too short and too clingy, similar knitted costumes for women were not introduced until well into the twentieth century. Typically a two-piece with vest and shorts, these early suits were cut and sewn from jersey knitted on circular machines. When public swimming became a mainstream activity, knitted swimsuits were widely adopted by all classes. Meanwhile, as skirts became shorter from the 1920s onwards, demand for women's stockings grew. They were a luxury item; in 1930, women bought just one or two pairs per year. Nylon stockings, introduced to the world by DuPont US in 1939 and knitted on machines capable of producing circular and fully fashioned fabric, were immediately popular. Glamorous, sheer and sexy, they were the practical alternative to silk.

Fig. 1.15 Made by John Smedley Ltd in the 1930s, this luxury swimsuit is better suited to sunbathing than swimming. The garment was cut and sewn from a panel of striped, lace, knitted fabric, produced on a straight-bar machine. PHOTOGRAPHER: PAM BROOK. COURTESY: JOHN SMEDLEY ARCHIVE CHARITABLE TRUST

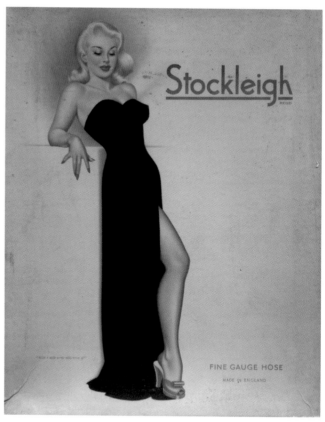

Fig. 1.16 This 1950s advertising material for Proper Pride nylon stockings with heel splicing, made by Stockleigh Hosiery Company, features an early illustration by the pin-up artist Archie Dickens. At 60 gauge, these were the sheerest seamed nylon stockings available at the time.

In the 1930s, women's fashion became more subtle and refined. Knitted fabrics with delicate lace designs were typical, while sweaters were fitted to the body. Pringle of Scotland emerged as the most innovative and influential of the cashmere mills, employing their own in-house designer, Otto Weisz. Weisz pioneered the new style of sweater and the ladies' twinset: a short-sleeved, plain sweater worn underneath a matching cardigan, which could be knitted in any of a wide range of yarns, from luxury cashmere and serviceable lambswool to the new man-made fibres.

After the outbreak of World War II, rationing limited the availability of clothing of all types. The government insisted that the knitted-outerwear trade reduce their output by 60 per cent. Many companies lost their premises and workforce, both of which were reassigned to war work. Those compan-

ies that remained groaned under the weight of government orders and the stipulations that must be followed. Despite its reduced resources, the Leicester-based Corah factory produced seventeen and a half million pairs of socks and stockings for the troops. The few articles that were produced for civilian wear were marked with a Utility mark that denoted regulation quality; the Utility scheme remained in place until 1952.

Post-war

Inspired by Christian Dior's New Look style and the elegant, modern Italian fashions of the day, the 1950s saw an emphasis on fully fashioned production. Expensive nylon stockings, being knitted on the newly imported American Reading

Fig. 1.17 Ribs knitted on a flatbed machine can be loaded by hand on to a transfer bar and transferred to a straight-bar machine for the body section to then be fully fashioned. This mid-twentieth-century production method is still in use today. COURTESY: JOHN SMEDLEY LTD

Fig. 1.18 Although this late-1950s cardigan from Marks & Spencer's St Michael brand is made from pure wool, man-made fibres were extensively used for fashion knitwear from that decade onwards.

knitting machines, were back in full production after the war. Along with the distinctive seams at the backs of the legs, they featured increasingly fancy details on the feet and heels. Men's lightweight slipovers, fully fashioned V-neck sweaters and polo shirts replaced waistcoats in many workplaces. Production of these styles, along with twinsets for women, kept the Cotton's machines busy, even as the market for woollen underwear declined.

By the mid-1960s, a new style of sweater had arrived: the skinny rib, popularized by Mary Quant, was boyish and chunky, with a high polo neck. It was easily mass-produced on powered flatbed machines, typically with acrylic yarn. This synthetic fibre had become widely used for knitwear during the 1950s as an easy-care alternative to wool. Around the same time, double-jersey polyester fabric knitted on machines capable of producing very fine-gauge circular rib became widespread, extending knitwear into areas of fashion previously reserved for woven fabrics such as suiting and trouser fabrics. The 1960s also saw the decline of the fully fashioned stocking; this once-iconic item felt impractical and old-fashioned in an era of miniskirts and bare legs. Tights, which covered up to the waist, were a practical and fashionable solution. Pretty Polly emerged as one of the most successful UK hosiery firms, successfully making the transfer to seamless production by investing in new, high-speed, Italian machines. By the late 1960s, sheer or woolly weft-knitted tights, along with lacy warp-knitted varieties, had become an essential part of a woman's wardrobe.

The 1960s was a period of significant change for the UK knitwear industry. Many of the long-established knitwear manufacturers, suffering from increased foreign competition, higher wage demands and changes in fashion, were taken over by the larger textile groups, such as Courtaulds, that had emerged. Despite these changes, fashion knitwear was hugely popular at all market levels, and employment in the UK industry was at its highest in the early 1970s. At this time, fashion and textiles students in the new polytechnics were increasingly experimenting with knitted fabrics and sharing knitting resources with the already well-established technical textile schools. A sound technical training for designers would equip them to apply their creativity to the realistic economic considerations of a high-volume, production-led UK industry.

In 1970, Scottish designer Bill Gibb won the coveted Dress of the Year award for his outfit featuring a hand-knitted waistcoat by Kaffe Fassett. This was an early indicator of a craft revival in high fashion that would gain momentum during the 1970s and 1980s. Gibb inspired other designers to overthrow conventions of mass-produced knitwear styles and to ruche, gather and drape knitted fabrics. Celebrated European fashion knitwear designers, such as Sonia Rykiel and the Missonis, further raised the profile of knitwear, firmly placing it within the international fashion system. In 1977, the first Pitti Filati trade event was held in Florence, helping Italian spinners to emerge as the most innovative and fashion-conscious.

The 1980s onwards

The 1980s saw the rejection of the man-made fibres that had been so heavily used in the preceding decades, as natural fibres, especially cotton, regained favour. The popularity of heritage styles meant that Scottish knitwear maintained its status, including the export of luxury garments made from cashmere or Sea Island cotton to booming markets in the USA and Far East. A trend – especially in Japan – for intricate, novelty knits provided work for hand-powered intarsia-knitting machines in Scottish mills until the end of the 1980s. Meanwhile, English knitwear designers who championed craft skills and natural yarns were growing in status internationally. Joseph's London fashion store featured expensive hand knits by Martin Kidman, while Nancy Vale produced nostalgic hand knits for Ralph Lauren and Calvin Klein. At her company's height in 1985, London-based designer Edina Ronay employed 2,000 home knitters. However, hand knitting's return to commercial production was short-lived; by the 1990s, hand-knitted garments that were produced in the UK had become too expensive to be viable. Other designers offered an alternative take on knitwear during the 1980s. BodyMap's outlandish garment shapes and iconic performance fashion pieces were achieved by using new yarns combining viscose and elastane in weirdly patterned, stretchy knitted fabrics, innovatively cut in a way that was both irreverent and unforgettable. Tunisian fashion designer Azzedine Alaïa's garments were sexy, awe-inspiring and edgy. He pushed the stretch potential of knitted fabric to the limit with supreme craftsmanship, in order to sculpt, squeeze and streamline the female body.

In 1982, a phenomenally successful new high street company, Next, was founded. Next's designers were adept at providing a colour-coordinated look across its ranges, including knitwear. For the first time in the context of mass production, the designer – rather than the manufacturer – was in control of what was produced. Other retailers followed suit, expanding their design teams and offering more choice to the customer through wider ranges and smaller orders. This shift was supported by a changing manufacturing environment, in which manufacturers were less able to dictate terms to the retailer, and by advances in knitting technology. In 1974, Stoll had introduced the first computerized flat-knitting machine; this machine could easily produce complex jacquard patterns and combinations of different stitch structures. In the 1980s, this technology was further enhanced with a graphical user interface providing the ability to programme designs visually, stitch by stitch and action by action. These innovations did not fully

Fig. 1.20 First developed in the 1980s, digital platforms with graphical user interfaces are used to programme knitwear designs visually, stitch by stitch and action by action.
COURTESY: JACK MASTERS LTD

replace existing technologies; computerized knitting machines required a considerable investment, and many companies retained machinery that still worked well for the production of classic lines.

The knitwear industry saw a downturn in the 1990s, driven by a number of factors – not least the vagaries of fashion. Power dressing favoured the suit over the sweater; this style was followed by almost total adoption by both sexes of the fleece (a casual, lightweight jacket made from polar-fleece fabric) in preference to the sweater in the mass market. The decade also saw the rise of performance fabrics and the increased use of elastomeric yarns, spun with viscose or wool, to create body-hugging knitwear. A global recession and changes to British export regulations also took their toll on the British industry. Knitwear manufacture rapidly became globalized, with China leading the way in terms of overseas production. China's lower labour costs and investment in advanced technology combined to produce a capability for producing low-cost, mass-produced knitwear with which no UK manufacturer could compete; other Asian countries such as Vietnam, Thailand and Bangladesh soon followed suit. The decision by Marks & Spencer to retract their long-held commitment to British manufacturing had a catastrophic impact on the companies that had supplied them almost exclusively. Consequently, many long-established British knitwear companies closed or were forced to reconfigure their business models, to become suppliers rather than manufacturers.

As a result of these changes, the roles of the knitwear designer and knitwear technologist shifted; where they had once been embedded in the British manufacturing environment, they were now either based within the head offices of retail companies or located overseas in the new centres of production. New opportunities opened up during these uncertain times: in the late 1980s and early 1990s, swatch-design studios emerged, selling exclusive designs by in-house and freelance designers to international clients.

Knitwear today

With knitwear back in fashion in recent years, much attention has been given to the traditional roots of knitwear and especially the heritage and skills of Scottish knitting in its broadest sense. The European fashion houses have been emulating the distinctive and highly crafted knitwear of the past for a new generation, using high-specification flatbed machines that can knit up to forty different colours in their intarsia mode of production. Pringle has emerged as the most talked-about British brand, building on their phenomenal 200-year knitwear heritage. Meanwhile, a new generation of directional designers have continued to move knitwear forward. Swedish designer Sandra Backlund's sculpted and huge-scale hand knits, for example, caught the attention of the press in the early twenty-first century and inspired a new crop of emerging designers to take up their knitting needles. Influential British brand Sibling and designer Carlo Volpi have also led the way with their playfully coloured, outsized and often mischievous take on traditional knitting.

Key innovations in technology have enabled the knitting of seamless garments, finally matching a capacity of hand knitting that has been practised for centuries. Building upon its expertise in seamless-glove manufacture, in 1995, Japanese company

Fig. 1.21 Jane Gaugain was one of the earliest knitting-pattern authors. The few illustrations at the beginning of her book *The Lady's Work Book* (1842) leave much to the imagination of the knitter.

A Lady's Golfing Jersey.

Fig. 1.22 In the late nineteenth century, *Weldon's Practical Needlework* featured a hand-knitting pattern for this ladies' golfing sweater. Unusually for knitwear of this period, this is an outerwear garment, with its sleeves following the fashionable style of the day.

Shima Seiki introduced its groundbreaking Wholegarment technology, a flatbed seamless machine that can produce an entire sweater in one operation. Italian hosiery-machine manufacturer Santoni has led the way in terms of developing machines for seamless circular knitting, responding to the continued demand for performance fabrics and moving into the growing sportswear market. Both technologies largely eliminate labour costs, enabling a return to onshore production, close to the target market.

Another landmark development in terms of fashion knitwear is the development of the knitted sports shoe; in 2011, after several years in development, Nike brought out their Flyknit sneaker. Cleverly utilizing the three-dimensional knitting potential of flatbed machines, the design vastly reduces the number of shoe-manufacturing processes required, resulting in a performance product that is lightweight, fashionable and highly technical. Today, we can be clothed from head to toe in knitwear; this versatile fabric has never been more prominent in our wardrobes.

Hobby knitting

Alongside the commercial knitwear industry, hand knitting has been pursued as a hobby since the Victorian era. Throughout this time, designers have produced patterns and instructional materials to support the making of fashionable items at home. A recent resurgence of activity, supported and enabled by the Internet, has brought new life to this age-old craft.

From industry to hobby

Although the mid-nineteenth century saw the demise of hand knitting as an industry, during the same period, the craft emerged as a leisure activity for the educated classes. Socially, there was an important distinction between knitting useful items to sell – historically, the province of the poor – and knitting as a hobby. Therefore, to ensure respectability, the new leisure knitters were encouraged to focus on 'fancy knitting', such as that involving intricate lace stitches for decorative doyleys and beaded knitting for purses and bags. During the late 1830s, the first instructional knitting publications and knitting patterns (then called receipts) appeared and were instantly popular. These early knitting resources were small volumes that provided written instruction and a few hand-coloured illustrations; the terminology was by no means standardized, as we expect today, and left a lot to the imagination in many cases. They also promoted a refined and dainty new way of holding the needles.

As the nineteenth century progressed, attitudes changed, and the knitting of useful items was encouraged for all. In addition to patterns for babies' and children's clothes, instructions for knitted jerseys, vests and socks for men and warm spencers (knitted jackets worn as underwear) for women appeared. Around the late 1870s, as the population became increasingly literate, the market for written knitting patterns grew. Magazines began to include patterns; cheaper *Penny Knitter* pamphlets were also produced. The monthly series *Weldon's Practical Needlework*, produced from 1886, included the first quality patterns to be published on a large scale, featuring a wide range of knitted and crocheted items. By the end of the nineteenth century, both boys and girls were taught practical hand knitting in schools, as part of basic home economy for poorer families.

Yarn spinners responded to the needs of the emergent hobby-knitting market. The first leisure knitters used fine, coloured wools imported from Germany, known as Berlin wool. Shetland wool was also appreciated for its fine quality and softness and was used extensively for fine lace shawls. Writers of the period refer to Lady Betty's wool: fleecy, softly spun, British wool, often used for petticoats and underwear. The first major English yarn spinner to supply hobby knitters was J.J. Baldwin, based in Halifax in West Yorkshire. Founded in 1785, the company expanded dramatically during the mid-nineteenth century to meet the high demand. They realized that, by publishing patterns for their own yarns, they would further stimulate demand, and their publication, *Woolcraft*, became a hugely influential knitters' bible. Baldwin's head designer,

Marjory Tillotson, was a major influence on pattern design, with a career spanning fifty years.

The modern era

In the early twentieth century, the popularity of knitted outerwear garments led to an increasing number of patterns being published for sweaters, cardigans, sporting jerseys and jackets. During World War I, British knitters were mobilized to produce items for the troops; comforts for soldiers and sailors included socks, stockings and mittens. During World War II, women of all ages, organized into official working parties, produced vast numbers of homemade items for the troops. By this time, regulation pattern books were being published to standardize what was made. As might be expected, there was a drive to teach people to knit during these periods. Women and girls often became expert knitters and continued to make items for themselves and their families after the war.

The supply of yarns and patterns for home knitters continued to develop during the first half of the twentieth century. J.J. Baldwin joined forces with a well-established Scottish spinner, John Paton, Son and Co., in the 1920s to become the world-famous Patons and Baldwins. By this time, knitting patterns supplied by yarn manufacturers had become the norm. In 1932, the company introduced the first monthly needlework magazine, *Stitchcraft*; its patterns responded to the latest fashions and had high-impact, colourful covers. During the following decades, a number of influential knitting writers and designers emerged. One of the most important was Mary Thomas, a fashion journalist and prolific writer on the subject of needlework. Aiming to inform the knitter about the cultural significance of knitting, Thomas travelled extensively to research historical knitted garments. James Norbury, a prolific designer, lecturer and writer, was the most influential hand-knitting designer of the 1950s; he became head designer for Patons and Baldwins in 1946. Norbury pioneered the use of Aran knitting styles for home knitters and encouraged a return to the traditional ways of holding the needles.

In the 1960s, as fashions of ready-made knitwear changed, new hand-knitting styles appeared. Patterns from the period show that chunky, brightly coloured hand knits were fashionable, often made in man-made yarns. Many patterns became noticeably simpler, catering for a new fashion-conscious but less-experienced knitter. *Vogue* and *Elle* magazines carried patterns in the latest styles. Patricia Roberts, one of the most influential and successful designers to emerge during this period,

Fig. 1.23 The popularity of knitwear in the 1980s led to an explosion of publishing for hand and machine knitters. Designers, such as Kaffe Fassett, authored sumptuously illustrated pattern books.

went against the trend for simplicity. Her youthful patterns were featured in magazines such as *19* and *Honey* for teenagers and, by the late 1970s, she had authored a range of books dedicated to her complex designs.

As hand-knitted garments proliferated on the catwalks during the 1980s, the craft of hand knitting once again enjoyed a surge in popularity. Versions of high-fashion styles were featured as patterns in fashion magazines and books. Complex picture knits, requiring considerable skill to knit, were common, as were chunky and boxy 'quick knits' made in natural yarns. Rowan Yarns, a company established in Yorkshire in 1978, was instrumental in spreading the art of hand knitting internationally. Founded by textiles graduate Stephen Sheard and his partner Simon Cockin, it initially offered a supply service to designers wanting contemporary yarns made of natural fibres. By working in this way, they forged relationships with the most talented British knitwear designers, such as Kaffe Fassett, Jean Moss, Sasha Kagan and Kim Hargreaves, who would later contribute designs to Rowan's books and magazines. These inspirational publications feature beautifully photographed and stylish garments, challenging techniques and artistic patterns.

Home knitting was not confined to hand knitting; specially developed domestic knitting machines, often called family knitters, were produced from the mid-nineteenth century onwards. During the 1950s, lightweight and versatile plastic machines, similar to the domestic knitting machines available today, appeared. These machines were tailored specifically for the hobby knitter and were made by a range of different manufacturers, mainly in Japan. During the following decades, the machines were developed to their full potential, with additional attachments and carriages enabling structures such as intarsia, ribs and lace to be knitted. The advent of computerized programming brought further technical possibilities. The 1980s was the heyday of the domestic machine; new publications targeted at the machine knitter, providing patterns and tips on technique, supplemented the traditional machine manufacturer's instruction manual. The tagline of one title, *Machine Knitting Monthly*, neatly summarizes the appeal of the domestic machine for many of its users: 'the hand-knitted look in a fraction of the time'. Machine-knitting clubs sprang up, aiming to provide encouragement and support for the new enthusiasts.

Fig. 1.24 Textile artist Rachael Matthews opened the London yarn shop Prick Your Finger in 2007, selling yarns from across the British Isles and hosting popular hand knitting and crochet workshops. PHOTOGRAPHER: ANTRANIG BASMAN

The contemporary resurgence

During the 1990s, there was a visible decline of interest in both hand and machine knitting. Handcrafted knitwear went out of fashion, and, as ready-made clothes became cheaper, the expense of making at home was off-putting for many people. UK spinners went out of business, knitting patterns were dropped from fashion magazines, yarn shops closed and department stores reduced their ranges of yarns.

Yet this decline was followed by a striking resurgence of hand-knitting activity, beginning in the early twenty-first century. Various reasons for this resurgence have been identified, including a growing appetite for hands-on craft activities and an increasing interest in sustainable living. Many new knitters have been motivated to make for themselves because of concerns over both the waste generated by the contemporary fast-fashion system and the conditions of workers producing these garments. Perhaps the most significant factor in the new hobby-knitting culture is the Internet; knitters are using the Web to connect to and inspire one another, as well as to access resources and materials. Blogs and social media enable individual knitters to share their projects, while YouTube provides instant video instruction for both basic and complex techniques.

The Web has also dramatically opened up opportunities for small-scale companies, leading to the emergence of a great wave of independent yarn producers and pattern designers. Ravelry, the social network for knitters, has been particularly influential in this regard. It allows designers to sell their patterns independently of the large spinners and publishers. This explosion of online activity has led to many offline initiatives; new knitting groups, yarn shops and regional yarn festivals have been created to meet the increased demand, along with a reinvigorated range of books and magazines becoming available.

CHAPTER 2

RESEARCH

by Claire Preskey

Introduction

Research underpins the entire design process and supports you, the designer, to develop new and original ideas. It provides the foundations for your thinking and a starting point for the creative journey. The diverse range of information that you compile and analyse when responding to a brief will inform your initial creative direction, provide a stimulus to push your designs further, and establish a context for your final outcomes. The quality of research and the way in which it feeds into the finished designs are major factors in the success of any design initiative. Yet research should not be confined to an individual project; a good designer will continually undertake research in order to keep up to date with developments in both the industry and the wider world that impact their work.

Research can be split into two categories: primary and secondary. Primary research involves interacting with objects, places and people and making first-hand observations through methods such as drawing, photography and note-taking.

Secondary research depends on information that has already been processed and edited by someone else – in books, magazines and exhibitions, for example. This research can broaden your horizons, enabling you to draw on sources that you could not otherwise access. The distinction between primary and secondary research is somewhat blurry; for example, you might use drawing to record your experiences of an exhibition and therefore generate original material from which to design.

This chapter covers various aspects of research, from the initial brief to the communication of a design concept, including market research, trend research and the gathering of personal inspiration.

The design brief

In your education and career as a designer, you are likely to have the opportunity to engage with a variety of briefs, whether driven by commercial needs or personal inspiration.

This display in the trend area at the Pitti Filati trade show in Florence links art to the development of knitted fabrics.

Analysing the brief

At the start of a design project, you should dissect the brief to understand what is being asked for; particular requirements are likely to be included. You may find that you have wide scope for creative freedom or that there are specific constraints within which you must work. For example, you may be asked to design for a specific market level or a particular brand and for a particular season; there may be a requirement for specific materials or manufacturing techniques to be used. A brief may ask you to address a particular trend or even to work to particular expectations in terms of durability. It will specify the outcomes to be generated, whether a range of knitted fabric samples or a collection of fully developed garment designs. Ask the following questions of any brief:

- Who are you designing for?
- What is the market level?
- What season are you designing for?
- What outcomes are needed?
- Are there any other specific requirements?

Thinking in this way will provide a direction for your research. Different briefs will require different kinds of research, as discussed in the later sections of this chapter. For certain projects, you might need to undertake targeted research into areas discussed in other chapters of this book, such as fibres and yarns, knitting technologies or manufacturing processes.

It is important to note that the brief will remain relevant throughout each stage of the design process and should be referred to at regular intervals. As you start to experiment with design ideas and explore a range of design outcomes, you should allow yourself time to pause and reflect upon your progress. Consult the brief and check that you are working within any constraints. This process of pause and reflection is essential for the success of your project.

Commercial briefs

Many briefs are commercially driven, requiring the designer to produce a range or collection for a specific brand or market level. Such briefs will be encountered by designers working in diverse industry-based roles, from in-house designers to free-lancers and those working for overseas suppliers. Commercial briefs typically provide numerous guidelines, such as indicating the target season, customer, occasion and cost restrictions. The designer's challenge is to create original designs while working within these commercial constraints. The degree of freedom will vary; for example, you may be given a specific colour palette to work with or you may be asked to develop a palette that is based on your research into the market and forthcoming season. While you will engage with a variety of types of research when working to a commercial brief, understanding the market level and the customer will be very important. Trend research is also likely to be crucial, providing direction in terms of silhouette, colour, stitch and pattern.

Some commercial briefs are much more open-ended. For example, a swatch designer may be commissioned to promote a spinner's new collection of yarns or showcase innovative designs in the trend section of an international trade fair. This type of brief offers great potential for the exploration of new ideas; research is likely to involve long-term trend forecasting and the gathering of inspiration in order to create an original concept.

Personal briefs

Self-directed designers, such as independent designer-makers or freelance swatch designers, may have the creative freedom to set their own briefs. While this may seem like an ideal situation, it can be challenging, as the designer is required to make many more decisions. In order to stay focused throughout the creative journey, when setting a personal brief, it is important to establish your aims, objectives and intended outcomes. The brief may include considerations that are also presented in commercial briefs, such as the intended customer, market level and season. As part of the process, you will need to identify and analyse the motivation underpinning the project. For example, a design initiative may be driven by a personal desire to explore a topic in depth, such as an artist, historical period or particular style of architecture. It could be driven by a process or material; you may find yourself wanting to understand the possibilities of a particular knitting technique or how a certain yarn behaves. Identifying this motivation and any other specific requirements will help you to consider the most productive types of research to undertake.

KEY TRENDS: RAW DATA – PITTI FILATI S/S 2018 GLITCH – TEXTILE VIEW SUBVERTED CLASSICS [FREE STYLE] – WGSN AW 19/20

These global thinking trends offer an interpretation of the world we live in today, focusing on technology and digital systems. The trend focuses on connections and how we have grown to depend on technology within all aspects of our lives. The 'Glitch' trend explores errors within systems, and the creation of irregular, unsymmetrical pattern.

CONTEXT: PATTERN FOCUSED

My final silhouette designs will be kept simple and will focus on classic shapes. Silhouette will be influenced by my swatch patterns, which will be the main focus. Contrasting yarns from lambswool to tape yarn will be used to create a high-end feel.

DESIGN RESPONSIBILITY: GENDER NEUTRAL, PATTERN FOCUSED RATHER THAN SILHOUETTE

The colour palette is gender neutral, the colours are bright and graphic and can be composed to create different moods. Silhouette will be simple and will focus on pattern, however some more detailed features such as decorative buttons and pockets will be featured to create a high-end feel. The collection is designed for longevity.

MARKET LEVEL: HIGH END BRIDGE BRAND – JOSEPH / ADER ERROR

I have chosen Joseph as my market level as they produce high quality knitwear but do not compromise on pattern. They also use prints across both male and female ranges and this will be a focus within my designs. Ader Error use simple silhouettes and similarly explore gender neutral knitwear.

VISUAL RESEARCH:

Graphic modern cityscapes, looking at contrasting lines and surface textures. I have utilised my own imagery from a trip to London, my images specifically focus on buildings around the TATE Modern area.

Collage, pattern, repeat, cut out, layering, wax resist, graphic shapes, glitch details.

KNITTED FABRIC AIMS: GENDER NEUTRAL, COLOUR AND PATTERN FOCUSED

For my final swatch collection, I will be exploring a range of techniques to depict glitch errors. These include partial knitting to create bold shapes, punching my own pattern cards to create distorted fair isles and using weaving to add layers of colour.

PERSONAL RESEARCH: GLITCH ARTISTS AND ILLUSTRATORS

I have researched artists from the trends who focus on the idea of glitching pattern. This has helped inform my visual research, looking at graphic mark making and bold use of colour.

COLOUR PALETTE: AW 19/20 COLLECTION

My colour palette inspiration has come from Textile View's Glitch Trend and Pitti Filati's Raw Data trend. These offered similarities and have a bold and fresh feel, with darker accents to bring it into autumn winter.

PLANNED OUTCOMES:

12–14 final samples exploring a combination of techniques to create contrast between graphic pattern and glitched movement.

Fig. 2.1 A personal brief establishes the designer's aims, objectives and intended outcomes. DESIGNER: KATE WARRINGTON

In education

If you are studying fashion knitwear design at college or university, you will be set a range of briefs to address during your course. Some will be personal briefs, while others will be much more commercial; you may even have the opportunity to work on live projects, in collaboration with industrial partners. Some projects will be very open, while in other cases you may be given a specific concept to research and explore through design development. Whatever the situation, the briefs that you are working with should allow you to develop your research, design, technical and transferable skills, and to build your knowledge of the various aspects of fashion knitwear design. Your ability to communicate the breadth of your primary and secondary research will be an important part of the assessment. Ensure that you understand what is being asked of you, and remember to keep referring to the brief as your project develops.

Market research

Market research develops your understanding of who you are designing for, in order to design fabrics and garments that will meet their needs. This can involve studying existing ranges, as well as thinking in detail about the customers who will ultimately wear your designs. By undertaking this type of research, you will be able to make informed decisions throughout the design process.

Studying existing ranges

Preparing a shop report involves observing the range on offer in a particular store. This may be a detailed report looking a specific brand; it may also cover the brand's competitors in order to understand what is available to the customer.

INTERIOR AESTHETIC

The store layout is clean, simple and easy to navigate. It consists of eye level clothing rails made from metal pipes. This reflected the brands contemporary edge.

Fig.10.

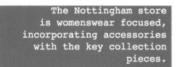

The Nottingham store is womenswear focused, incorporating accessories with the key collection pieces.

Fig.11.

Fig. 2.2 This page from a shop report on a contemporary brand examines the store aesthetic.
REPORT: KATE WARRINGTON

Alternatively, if you are designing for a particular market level rather than an individual brand, a comparative shop report of a range of relevant brands will offer a good starting point. Once you have developed your market knowledge, you may find that you need to undertake further research, for example, investigating relevant trends.

While some information can be gleaned from a brand's website, it is important to visit the store, if possible, as you will learn a great deal by examining the garments up close. Details such as the manufacturing processes used for a garment and the garment's quality will not be evident online. Touching a garment will offer you a sense of the fabric handle, whereas trying it on will offer a sense of intended fit. However, be aware that your local store may not stock the full range; in this case, a combination of in-store and online research may be most appropriate.

Some stores may be happy for you to take photographs of their knitwear; if not, having a small notepad handy will allow you to jot down key findings. Making small thumbnail sketches of garment silhouettes, trim details and stitch patterns will provide a reminder of what you have seen. The following lists of prompts indicate the types of observations that you should be making. In all cases, pay attention both to the range of different options available and to the proportion of each option within the range. For example, when looking at the gauges of knitted fabrics used, you might note that the store offers both chunky- and fine-gauge fabrics but that around two-thirds of the knitwear garments fall within the chunky category.

Select accessories were displayed above the rails, creating outfit ideas and encouraging the impulse consumer to make a purchase.

Fig.12.

Lower level tables displaying accessories were situated at the front of the store, making it feel open.

Fig.14.

Large images of the Autumn Winter campaign helped section the store. They also complement the clothing below, which are arranged into colour stories.

Fig.13.

12

Fig. 2.3 Examining the use of promotional imagery in-store helps the designer to understand a brand's identity and target customer. REPORT: KATE WARRINGTON

Study the current range of knitted fabrics within the store, identifying:

- Colour palettes: a range of palettes across the store, a specific palette made up of core and accent colours?
- Fibre contents: wool, cashmere, mohair, alpaca, cotton, silk, acrylic, viscose?
- Yarn types: smooth, textured, airy, tweed, slub, bouclé, chenille, tape, lurex?

- Gauges of knitted fabrics: chunky (2.5–4 gauge), mid (5–8 gauge), fine (10–21 gauge); hand knitting; crochet?
- Basic structures: single jersey, ribs, cardigan, milano?
- Complex structures: tuck patterns, miss stitches, lace, partial knitting, purl fabrics, cables?
- Colourwork: stripes, Fair Isle, plating, jacquards, intarsia?
- Any embellishments: printing, beading, sequins, embroidery?

KEY FEATURES

METAL HARDWARE
RING DETAIL

LACE UP
SLEEVES

RING ZIP
CUFF
DETAILS

Fig.73.

BUTTON
DETAILS

Fig.74.

Fig.75.

Fig.76.

RETRO SPORTS FEEL | TEXTURAL | REPETITION

Fig. 2.4 Finishing details are important components of knitwear designs and should be studied as part of a detailed shop report. REPORT: KATE WARRINGTON

Study the current range of knitwear garments within the store, identifying:

- Manufacturing processes: fully fashioned, cut-and-sew, seamless?
- Knitwear silhouettes: fitted, oversized, asymmetric, boxy?
- Armhole and sleeve styles: set-in sleeve, saddle shoulder, raglan, kimono; short, long, three-quarter-length sleeve?
- Neckline styles: V-neck, crew neck, scoop neck, turtleneck, polo neck, collar, shawl collar, cowl?
- Trim details: rib trim, sandwich trim, scalloped-edge trim, strapping?

- Hardware: zip fastenings, buttons, D-rings?
- Details: pockets, drawstrings, tie fastenings, belts, woven trims?

While in the store, try on garments to understand their fit. Construction details can be observed by turning the garment inside out and looking to see where the seams are placed. If you have a tape measure with you, you can measure the sleeves, neckline drop and body length, to get an accurate recording of the scale of a garment.

Finally, study the range as a whole, considering:

- How many knitwear pieces are in the range in total?
- What are the price points?
- What is the size range?
- Can any key basics within the knitwear range be identified?
- How are the garments merchandised?
- What is the aesthetic of the store?

In addition to your in-store research, you should research the way in which the brand promotes itself. Online research will be particularly useful here, enabling you to study the brand's advertising campaigns and social-media presence. This will provide a valuable insight into the brand and how it is marketed; in turn, this will help you to develop relevant fabric and garment designs that capture the brand's aesthetic. Trade journals can also be a valuable source of market research, providing information on sales patterns across different market levels and consumer buying trends. These reports can help you to identify what is selling well; this knowledge will inform your decisions when designing for a particular market level or specific commercial client. For example, a report may indicate that classic staples are selling well compared to high fashion or that embellished knitwear is starting to grow in popularity.

Analysing your findings

Through analysis of your observations, you should be able to gain a much clearer understanding of the brand, which will help you to generate appropriate designs. Start to analyse your findings by looking at the collection as a whole. Are you able to identify common styles, necklines, sleeve shapes and lengths? Once you have understood garment shape and style, you can apply the same analysis to colour and pattern. Your findings should reveal how the brand builds their collections. They will also provide evidence of the brand's approach to design. For example, if you have a good knowledge of current trends, you should be able to discern whether the brand's range is a derivative of catwalk designs or guided by a more original design identity. You should also be able to discover how the brand interprets popular trends. For example, it may respond to a sportswear trend by incorporating obviously sporty details directly into the brand's knitwear designs, or the connection may be much more subtle. Combining this information with trend research and/or your own

concept will enable you to create a range that is suitable for the brand, while not replicating their current offer.

When responding to a commercial brief, cost will be particularly important; by studying existing ranges, you will be able to select appropriate materials, manufacturing techniques and details such as embellishments and trims. A customer buying a garment at a higher price point will be looking for a higher-quality fabric handle and therefore you may be able to consider using a pure merino wool or cashmere yarn. By contrast, a garment at a lower price point would be produced by using a pure or blended acrylic yarn.

Understanding the customer

Identifying and understanding the customer – the people who will ultimately wear your designs – is as important as gaining an understanding of your market; the two coexist. By starting to build a picture of who the customer is, you will be able to make informed decisions about aspects such as the shape, finish and materials of your designs. An important element of this picture is the customer's lifestyle, which will determine what they wear and therefore what they buy. For example, a professional who travels a lot may require a combination of formal wear and smart-casual wear that is easy to pack and readily adapts to different climates. You should consider their preferences, both in terms of fashion and more widely. What other brands do they buy? What is their home like? How do they spend their leisure time? Where do they go on holiday? What music and films do they like? The age and life stage of the customer will also be of interest. A younger person may have different spending priorities to someone with family commitments.

While a brand's range and promotion will provide a strong indication of the customer that it is seeking to target, to develop a first-hand understanding, it is a good idea to observe shoppers in the store. As designer Genevieve Sweeney explains, 'I watch what customers are buying, which items they pull off a rail and what stops them in their path. It is such an easy and powerful way to understand who the customer is.' If you are working to a personal brief, it may be useful to think about a specific consumer tribe: a group of people with a shared philosophy or lifestyle that shapes their taste preferences and consumption behaviours. For example, a tribe may have a strong ethical stance and interest in personal well-being that leads to a preference for local and organic products. Again, observing or even speaking directly to individual customers will provide valuable insight into their preferences and motivations.

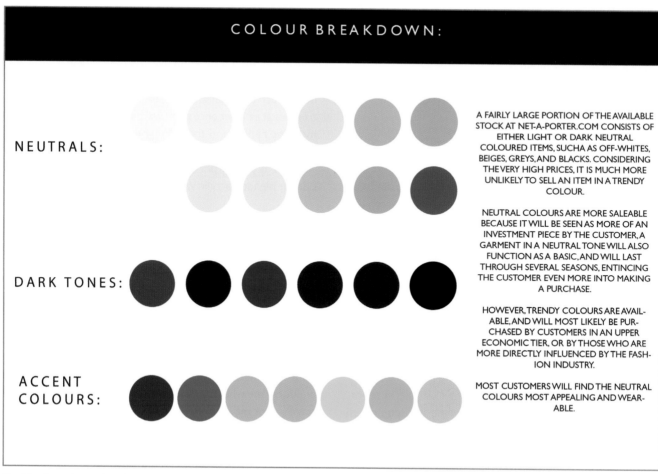

COLOUR BREAKDOWN:

NEUTRALS:

A FAIRLY LARGE PORTION OF THE AVAILABLE STOCK AT NET-A-PORTER.COM CONSISTS OF EITHER LIGHT OR DARK NEUTRAL COLOURED ITEMS, SUCHA AS OFF-WHITES, BEIGES, GREYS, AND BLACKS. CONSIDERING THE VERY HIGH PRICES, IT IS MUCH MORE UNLIKELY TO SELL AN ITEM IN A TRENDY COLOUR.

NEUTRAL COLOURS ARE MORE SALEABLE BECAUSE IT WILL BE SEEN AS MORE OF AN INVESTMENT PIECE BY THE CUSTOMER, A GARMENT IN A NEUTRAL TONE WILL ALSO FUNCTION AS A BASIC, AND WILL LAST THROUGH SEVERAL SEASONS, ENTINCING THE CUSTOMER EVEN MORE INTO MAKING A PURCHASE.

DARK TONES:

HOWEVER, TRENDY COLOURS ARE AVAILABLE, AND WILL MOST LIKELY BE PURCHASED BY CUSTOMERS IN AN UPPER ECONOMIC TIER, OR BY THOSE WHO ARE MORE DIRECTLY INFLUENCED BY THE FASHION INDUSTRY.

ACCENT COLOURS:

MOST CUSTOMERS WILL FIND THE NEUTRAL COLOURS MOST APPEALING AND WEARABLE.

Fig. 2.5 By analysing the observations made in a shop report, an understanding of the brand's use of colour can be developed. REPORT: ALESSIA DE FRANCESCO

Presenting your market research

A shop report may be presented in a variety of ways, depending on the situation and the requirements of the brief. In a commercial context, an in-house designer may be asked to put together a board showing current competitor and market information. This would be a quick exercise to share research with other designers in the studio. A more formal option is to produce a visual report, collating all of the information that has been gathered. This may include screenshots from the brand's online presence, advertising campaigns, ethics mission statements, details of competitors, and photographs of the range and store environment. You may also include your own drawings of garments. If you are including a customer profile, you can use images and keywords to build a detailed picture of their lifestyle. You may wish to introduce your report with an overview of the brand and a brief outline of the brand's history. Another potential method is a visual slide show and verbal presentation.

Whatever the format, you need to demonstrate that you have developed a clear understanding of the range(s) that you have researched, and that you are aware of the brand's identity and target customer. Consider how you will order the information and visually communicate your research. Any accompanying text should be direct and to the point, highlighting specific observations that you have made. The reader should be able to scan the pages and be able to understand your key points swiftly.

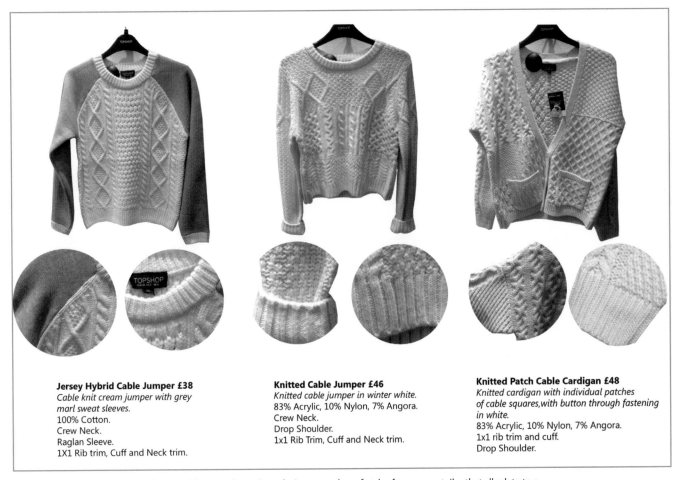

Jersey Hybrid Cable Jumper £38
Cable knit cream jumper with grey marl sweat sleeves.
100% Cotton.
Crew Neck.
Raglan Sleeve.
1X1 Rib trim, Cuff and Neck trim.

Knitted Cable Jumper £46
Knitted cable jumper in winter white.
83% Acrylic, 10% Nylon, 7% Angora.
Crew Neck.
Drop Shoulder.
1x1 Rib Trim, Cuff and Neck trim.

Knitted Patch Cable Cardigan £48
Knitted cardigan with individual patches of cable squares,with button through fastening in white.
83% Acrylic, 10% Nylon, 7% Angora.
1x1 rib trim and cuff.
Drop Shoulder.

Fig. 2.6 With this shop report, designer Shannon Green is analysing a number of styles from one retailer that all relate to a trend for cable fabrics. Details of price, fibre composition, structure and garment shape are all included. REPORT: SHANNON GREEN

Researching trends

An understanding of current and forthcoming trends is often an important element of the research that is needed when designing fashion knitwear. This understanding can be gained via trend-forecasting agencies and trade fairs or through the designer's own independent research.

Types of trends

An awareness of fashion trends, whether fleeting fads or slower shifts in style, enables the designer to create designs that feel up to date at the time that they reach the market. Designers working to commercial briefs must be able to recognize and anticipate shifts in colour, shape, texture and yarn, in order to ensure that their designs are current and have a place within the global fashion and textiles arena. To develop this awareness, it is necessary to appreciate the various ways in which trends emerge and spread. Many trends trickle down from international catwalks; designer collections have been a source of inspiration for mass-market fashions for decades and continue to have an influence. At the same time, trends can bubble up from street and youth culture, influencing both high street and designer collections.

Awareness of trends should not be confined to garment and textile designs; a good designer will keep abreast of the cultural events and social shifts that affect the lifestyles, tastes and motivations of the people for whom they are designing. The cultural zeitgeist can shape fashion trends. For example,

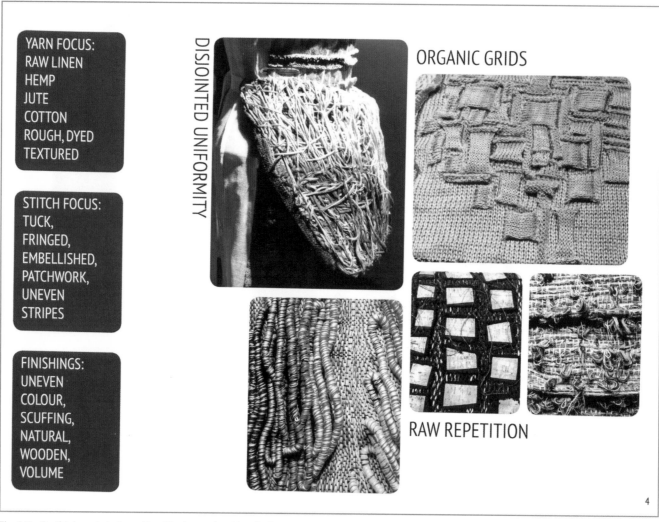

YARN FOCUS:
RAW LINEN
HEMP
JUTE
COTTON
ROUGH, DYED
TEXTURED

STITCH FOCUS:
TUCK,
FRINGED,
EMBELLISHED,
PATCHWORK,
UNEVEN
STRIPES

FINISHINGS:
UNEVEN
COLOUR,
SCUFFING,
NATURAL,
WOODEN,
VOLUME

DISJOINTED UNIFORMITY

ORGANIC GRIDS

RAW REPETITION

Fig. 2.7 On this board, designer Kate Warrington has identified an emergent knitwear trend. Keywords indicate relevant yarns, stitches and finishes.

on several occasions, depictions of the life and style of the artist Frida Kahlo in films and exhibitions have influenced the catwalk collections of established designers in the following seasons. At a deeper level, social, political and economic factors have an impact on our lives and therefore the ways in which consumers behave. Such influences may be primarily practical; for example, living in centrally heated and air-conditioned homes reduces the need for oversized, chunky sweaters, with people preferring to wear garments that they can layer in order to adapt to subtle changes in the environment. They may be less direct; during periods of economic recession, there is often an increased appetite for nostalgia, driving a desire for garments that remind us of the past.

One particularly important shift is the rising interest in sustainable fashion. The impact of fast fashion on the environment, and on the workers who produce the garments, has been widely reported in recent years. Some designers have responded, developing an understanding of the impacts of the garments that they produce and using sustainable design strategies that focus on factors including material choices, manufacturing methods, supply-chain transparency and both physical and emotional longevity. Similarly, as consumers have become increasingly aware of these issues, they have changed their buying behaviours; some people are now choosing to buy ethically sourced items and seek out garments that offer a timeless look and therefore will not fall out of fashion quickly.

Fig. 2.9 Garments in trend-forecasting displays help visitors to understand how yarns, colours and stitches will work on the body.

Fig. 2.8 The trend-forecasting areas within specialist knitwear-industry trade fairs, such as SpinExpo in Shanghai, present directional thinking in terms of yarn, colour, stitch, texture and shape.

Fig. 2.10 Spinners use shade cards to present their colour palettes for the coming season.

Trend forecasting and trade fairs

Forecasting companies undertake research to identify emerging trends. Such companies operate internationally, with their trendspotters across the globe reporting a variety of observations, from specific fashion and textiles trends to political and economic influences. Their observations can cover street style, street culture and youth movements in cities across the world. For example, a new music scene may spark a new movement in youth culture that then has the potential to spread through to mass-market fashion trends. The trendspotter must identify these emerging influences and determine whether they will remain niche or influence mainstream lifestyles. They also look to identify new consumer tribes, as discussed in a previous section.

Trendspotters report on store merchandising and examine both large, renowned stores and independent designer and vintage boutiques. Shop-window displays act as a three-dimensional mood board, where the selection of fashion products and their colours, textures and shapes can be a sign of new thinking. Trendspotters visit fashion shows, trade fairs and graduate shows, which can include other types of design such as product design and architecture. These shows provide the opportunity to encounter emerging ideas and new technical processes first-hand.

This information is analysed and used to produce coherent and concise reports for use by designers and other creatives. This service is valuable because it keeps the designer informed about global shifts and provides the designer with access to a wealth of carefully filtered information. Trend reports may be specific to a particular area of fashion and textiles, focusing on design considerations such as colour, texture or silhouette. Catwalk reports indicate which designers have been particularly influential in a given season, as well as identifying common threads between multiple collections. For example, it may be noted that there are a lot of pictorial knits on the catwalk for one season or that knitwear shapes are oversized. Other reports will have a much broader scope, analysing significant shifts in consumer behaviour or capturing the mood of what is filtering through into new thinking in design. Trend predictions are normally produced for Autumn/Winter and Spring/Summer collections, with smaller updates occurring within the season. Specialist fashion and textiles publications also offer up-to-date information relating to current trends. Designers analyse these reports and extract information that is relevant to their project; this can be used directly to inform designs or be interpreted much more loosely and used as a launch pad for the selection of personal inspiration.

Another useful source of trend-forecasting information is the specialist industry trade fairs that relate to the fashion knitwear industry. Most trade fairs include a dedicated fashion and fabric trend-forecasting area that presents directional thinking within knitwear design in terms of yarn, colour, stitch, texture and shape. Individual exhibitor stands also provide valuable information, with new yarn ranges being showcased through shade cards, sample books and garments. Because trade fairs bring together a wide variety of professionals, including designers, design studios, retail buyers, design agents, consultants, spinners and machinery manufacturers, they present an excellent opportunity to learn about developments in the industry and widen your professional network.

Undertaking your own trend research

While trend-forecasting companies provide a valuable service, access to their reports can be costly. With this in mind, designers – particularly those working independently – may wish to undertake their own trend research. As for the trendspotters working for the forecasting companies, this research could take many forms. It may involve primary research; the designer could produce a shop report, having examined the ranges of directional labels, and then use the findings to inform their own designs, or could visit a city with influential stores, to study the shop windows and interior merchandising. They may choose to study street fashion and youth culture by people watching at relevant events. Visits to exhibitions or watching films can provide creative inspiration as well as insights into emergent trends. Alternatively, information can be gathered via secondary research; for example, a designer may analyse catwalk collections, to generate their own original conclusions. They might use magazines, news media and online resources to identify new tribes, cultural movements, and social and political influences. Social media can be particularly valuable for keeping up to date with the latest thinking; fashion bloggers who attract a huge following provide a good indication of current and forthcoming tastes.

Gathering inspiration

The types of research discussed so far involve the designer looking outwards, to develop their understanding of the context within which their designs will sit. For many projects, and particularly those that respond to a personal brief, there is a need for another type of research: the gathering of a unique collection of inspirational material to create a strong design concept and inform the creative direction of the entire design process. This material will be used to inspire the choices of colours, materials, structures and shapes, and may lead to unexpected avenues of creative exploration. It should enable the designer to create an individual response to the design brief and come up with original and innovative final outcomes. The process of gathering and locating your inspiration should be exciting and engaging; this will encourage you to sustain your interest and motivation throughout the project.

Finding a theme

In order to start your search for inspiration, you need to identify a theme to work with. A theme may be specified in your brief; if your project is more open-ended then your research may help you to identify possible avenues. You may find that a recent exhibition or film sparks an idea, or you may have encountered an emerging trend in a trade-fair forecasting area that you wish to explore in more depth. In the early stages of your project, your theme may have a singular focus; alternatively, you may choose to investigate a collection of subtly connected ideas or to juxtapose contrasting concepts.

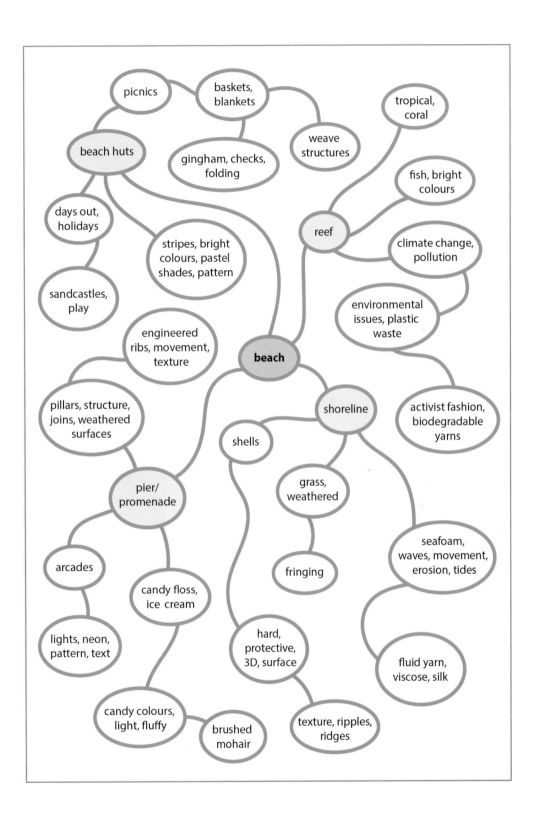

Fig. 2.11 A mind map can be used to identify multiple potential directions for research from a single starting point.

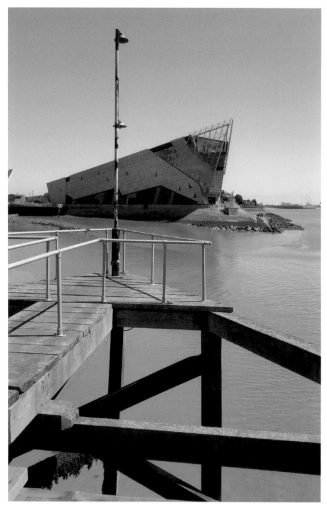

Fig. 2.12 Architectural structures, such as The Deep aquarium in Hull, can provide valuable inspiration for knitwear design.

Fig. 2.14 This image of pillars beneath a pier might inspire a designer to develop knitwear including engineered rib structures and deconstructed seams.

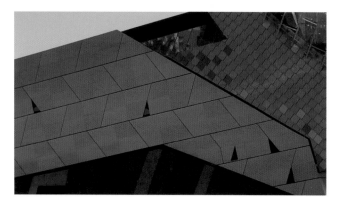

Fig. 2.13 The graphic lines, shiny surfaces and repetition that feature in this ultra-modern building could be used as inspiration to influence various aspects of knitted textiles.

Fig. 2.15 Designer Mollie French has used photography and drawing to document sporting events, taking inspiration from the movement of the body.

A mind map will help you to identify potential directions for your research. Start by identifying a word or phrase that represents your theme, then think of additional words that relate to it in different ways. By grouping these words, you will see connections that spark new ideas and suggest avenues of research in terms of imagery, colour, texture and shape. As your mind map develops, it is not unusual to discover that you have multiple themes and potential projects stemming from a single word; you will need to make decisions about the best direction to take. As you undertake research and document your own creative responses, further ideas will emerge, meaning that your theme will evolve and develop. This process will allow you to take ownership of your project and create an original response to your subject matter.

Nature has been an influence within design for centuries and offers an endless source of inspiration. From a peacock's plumage to the rocky cliffs of a remote coastline, the diversity of the natural world provides a wealth of material in terms of colours and textures. The built environment, too, can provide many potential themes to be explored, suggesting forms, materials, patterns and structures. Different types of building will offer different types of visual information. For example, Antoni Gaudí's Casa Milà will offer very different imagery to

that of the modern skylines of Dubai. Along with architecture, other types of art, craft and design are fertile areas for research, from the patterning on vintage crockery to the work of an influential sculptor. You may look to textiles and fashion for a starting point for your project; dress from another culture or from a specific historical period, for example, could provide a rich source of inspiration. While you might be instinctively drawn to look at knitwear for inspiration, other types of textiles and garments, such as prints and tailoring, will also have much to offer. Potential areas of focus range from the everyday clothes worn by working people and the dress associated with distinctive subcultures through to the work of iconic designers. A variation on this approach would be to look in detail at a particular person, whether contemporary, historical or fictional.

Sources of information

As you get stuck into your search for inspiration, you will be collecting material from a diverse range of sources. Different projects will require different approaches; some themes will involve a lot of primary research, while others will be explored most effectively through secondary research. Furthermore,

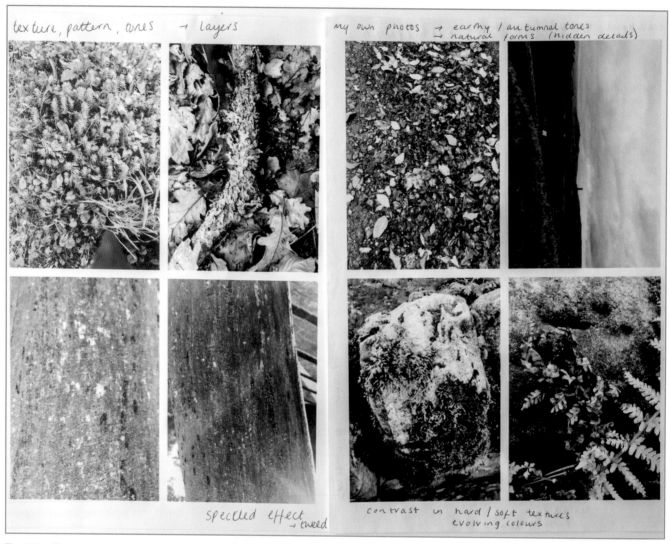

texture, pattern, tones → layers

my own photos → earthy / autumnal tones
→ natural forms (hidden details)

speckled effect
→ tweed

contrast in hard / soft textures
evolving colours

Fig. 2.16 Photography can be used as a primary research method, capturing natural textures to inspire choices of yarns and stitches. DESIGNER: ALICE RILEY

while a certain method of research may suit one designer, it will not necessarily suit another. It is up to you to develop an approach that works for you and your project.

Exploring objects, garments and artworks is a great way to gain inspiration at the beginning of a project. Aim to access original material wherever possible, rather than relying solely on images created by others. This will allow you to gain a deeper understanding of an item by observing detail, looking at it from different perspectives and perhaps handling it yourself. You might find thought-provoking objects in second-hand shops or even the family attic; alternatively, museums and specialist archives are a valuable source of research. Permanent and

temporary exhibitions offer the opportunity to view objects from diverse historical periods and cultures, while items not on display can often be accessed by appointment. In addition to the major national museums, you can visit smaller specialist archives with fascinating collections. Many archives have now been digitized and are therefore available online. If you are taking inspiration from aspects of the natural or built environment, visits to suitable locations – whether a windswept beach or a busy city street – will be of great value. Take photographs and use a sketchbook to capture your observations. You may also collect objects to take home and to construct a still life to draw from later. If you are researching a particular period in history,

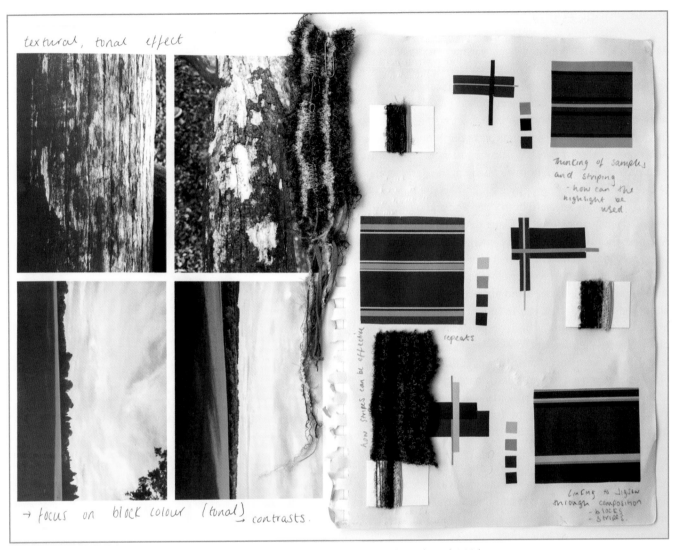

textural, tonal effect

thinking of samples and striping - how can the highlight be used.

how stripes can be effective

repeats

→ focus on block colour (tonal) contrasts.

linking to jigsaw through composition - blocks - stripes.

Fig. 2.17 As research is documented in the sketchbook, the designer can start to respond to it through initial design ideas. Here, stripe layouts are used to investigate colour and proportion. DESIGNER: ALICE RILEY

a trip to a historic building decorated in the appropriate style could provide another productive avenue.

If direct access to inspirational material is not possible or you wish to pursue another line of enquiry, you can turn to secondary research. This means searching through sources such as books and magazines, and searching online. An afternoon spent browsing in the library can be incredibly productive; finding specialist books on your theme should help you to deepen your understanding and to access high-quality imagery, while archives of past issues of magazines can provide a treasure trove of material. In addition to searching for material directly relating to your theme, you might consider looking for artists, photographers and designers who have worked with similar topics, in order to study their responses to the subject matter. Today, the Internet is probably the most accessible starting point for sourcing secondary research. In addition to websites, blogs and social media, you can access material such as films and documentaries. While the nature of online research means that valuable unanticipated information can be readily discovered, it is easy to get distracted and to head off on a tangent: aim to find a balance, by being open to new ideas while staying connected to your brief.

Documenting your inspiration

Research can be documented in many ways; you should choose the most effective method to suit your preferred way of working and your project. Secondary research will typically be gathered as copies or scans and can be compiled in a sketchbook or research file. Consider how the images link together, and collate them in an order that communicates your thought process. Add notes to record why a particular image is significant to your project. In terms of primary research, the designer has a choice of media. Photography is an immediate and popular way to document research. Both video and audio can also be recorded easily, to be used at a later date to influence design. Alternatively, research can be documented in a sketchbook by using drawing, collage and mark-making; these methods start to overlap with the creative responses to the research that start the design process, as discussed in Chapter 5. Think carefully about the approach that you will adopt. If a drawing is taken from a photograph then all decisions regarding the observation of the object – such as light, position and focus – have already taken place. Alternatively, if an object is drawn directly from life, it can be moved and touched, enabling design decisions to be made at the time that the marks are made.

As a designer, you may be fortunate enough to have a dedicated workspace or studio. If this is the case, you may use a wall or pinboard to display current inspiration. Throughout the design process, you may edit or add imagery, yarns and fabrics. As you develop your ideas, take photographs as a record of your design journey. The digital world offers virtual and portable alternatives that can make research exciting, instantaneous and accessible twenty-four hours a day. Whether used as an alternative to the sketchbook or as a complementary means of collating information, these approaches provide constant motivation and stimulus and enable the sharing of your project for instant feedback.

Communicating your concept

Once you have collated a wide range of primary and secondary visual research, potentially covering both emerging trends and your own personal inspiration, you are ready to finalize your design concept and communicate it via a concept board (also known as a mood board, storyboard or inspiration board). The concept board is essentially a collection of your most relevant and influential research. Once created, the concept board will serve as a reference throughout the design process.

Fig. 2.18 Use of an image-editing CAD app to manipulate photographs supports the exploration of visual research in the designer's sketchbook. DESIGNER: KATE WARRINGTON

Editing and selecting

Creating the concept board can be a challenging task, as it requires you to make decisions and edit your research, in order to focus on the most important elements. When selecting imagery for use on the board, ensure that each element has a purpose; try to avoid including multiple images that communicate the same idea. Another consideration is the aesthetic of the images. Those selected should link together visually and reflect the intended aesthetic of the range that you will go on to design. For example, if you have already decided that your fashion knitwear collection will have a structured look, you

Fig. 2.19 The designer's workspace can be used to assist the designer to visualize a design concept, by displaying inspiration images and yarn ideas. As the design process develops, the selection of imagery can be changed and fabric samples can be added. DESIGNER: SHAUNA MILLS

Fig. 2.20 When creating a concept board, the designer must edit their research to focus on the most important elements. Every image must have a purpose and communicate the intended aesthetic. DESIGNER: KATE WARRINGTON

should select images with an appropriate mood and feel. In addition to your imagery, you may wish to add tactile elements that provide an insight into potential design outcomes, such as yarn wrappings, colour chips, inspirational textures and initial stitch ideas. You may also wish to include keywords relating to your concept, taken from your mind map.

While putting together your board, reflect on your project brief and ensure that the concept will help you to meet its requirements. Be prepared to undertake further research and to reposition your concept, if necessary. Through the process of editing and selecting material for the concept board, it is not unusual to discover a gap within your research, which you will need to address before moving on. A good way of evaluating your concept board is to consider that it should inspire not only you but also the viewer. Could another designer work from your board? Does it provide a starting point for the design process and provide the right context in relation to your intended outcomes?

Presentation

There are many forms that a concept board can take, and your brief might define this. It may be digital and created through an image-editing app, such as Adobe Photoshop. Such a concept board can be printed out, with any tactile elements then being added. Working in this way enables you to send your board digitally or upload it to online platforms. Alternatively, the board could be created as a hard copy by using foam board or thick card. Depending on your project, you may feel the need to create more than one concept board. For example, you may create one board that captures influential primary and secondary research, with additional boards focusing on design-specific elements such as yarn, colour, silhouette and garment detailing. Ensure that key information is communicated on each board, such as the brand and season for which you are designing.

CHAPTER 3

YARNS

by Kandy Diamond

Introduction

Although yarn is the basis of all knitwear, designers often underestimate the importance of understanding yarns beyond their aesthetic values. The more you know about the origins, production and properties of yarns, the more effectively you will be able to design. This knowledge begins with fibres: the raw materials from which yarns are made. Whether natural or man-made, each fibre has its own unique characteristics at the microscopic level. These characteristics affect the way in which the fibre behaves – in terms of diverse factors such as surface appearance, drape, durability and warmth. The way in which the fibre is formed into a yarn adds further variables in terms of behaviour and performance.

Selecting yarns from the array of choices on offer can, therefore, be a challenging process. The designer must weigh up a range of considerations. For example, you might be simultaneously considering a yarn's textural finish, its suitability for a particular machine and its cost. In navigating yarn ranges, you need to understand the numerical systems that are used to indicate a yarn's thickness and construction. And, as sustainability becomes ever more important within the fashion industry, it is crucial that you are aware of the environmental impacts of

Part of the joy of knitwear design is working with the array of yarns that is available.

your materials, in order to make informed choices. This chapter unravels the world of yarn, from fibres through to sourcing, demystifying terms such as count and Z twist along the way.

Fibres

Yarns begin life as fibres, and these fibres come from a wide variety of origins, both natural and man-made. Natural fibres are either animal-based, such as wool and silk, or plant-based, such as cotton and linen. Historically, locally available natural fibres were used; the expansion of global trade brought about greater choice, while the introduction of man-made fibres from the late nineteenth century onwards further increased the options. There are two types of man-made fibres: synthetic fibres, made from carbon-based chemical compounds derived from oil and coal; and regenerated fibres, made from naturally occurring fibre-forming polymers. Natural and man-made fibres are often blended for reasons of cost, durability and aesthetics.

Fibres are categorized as either staple or filament. Staple fibres, such as wool, are short. Imagine a single strand pulled from a sheep's fleece: this is a single staple fibre. This single staple fibre is combined with many other staple fibres to form a yarn. In contrast, filament fibres are continuous lengths. Most synthetic fibres fall into this category, because of the way in which they are produced.

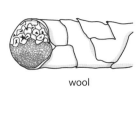
wool

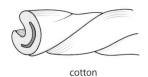
cotton

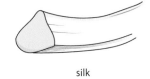
silk

Fig. 3.1 The characteristics of natural and man-made fibres are evident when viewed at a microscopic scale and affect the qualities of the yarns and fabrics created from them.

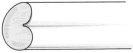
acrylic

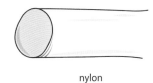
nylon

viscose

Fig. 3.2 This Herdwick lamb, Lonk sheep and two Angora goats are representatives of just some of the animals that are bred for their fleeces by Susan Crawford, a designer of knitwear and natural-fibre yarn, at her farm in Lancashire. PHOTOGRAPHER: DENIS BRICE

Fig. 3.3 Woolen fibres from different sheep breeds have evident aesthetic and textural differences. PHOTOGRAPHER: ISABEL BROWN

Natural fibres

Wool

This familiar fibre, closely associated with knitwear, primarily comes from sheep and has many variants, such as lambswool, extra-fine merino wool and wool of various specialist breeds. In addition, fibres from other animals including goat (cashmere and mohair), llama and alpaca, as well as camel and yak, are also classified as wools. Wool is naturally renewable and bio-degradable, breaking down quickly and easily when buried and providing the soil with nutrients. With the increasing import-ance of sustainable practices in the fashion and textiles industry, these properties are now being recognized and promoted.

Wool is a staple fibre, with a distinctive scaly surface. These scales give the yarn its unique felting potential – activated by a combination of water, heat and agitation – and are the reason that you must not put your best cashmere sweater on a hot wash! Wool also has a unique molecular structure that makes the fibre act like a spring, being capable of stretching up to 50 per cent when dry and 30 per cent when wet. Because yarns are stretched and manipulated both in production and in wear, this property helps woollen knitted garments to retain their shape.

The unique structure of the wool fibre means that it acts as an insulator in cold weather, but it can also draw moisture away from the body, helping to cool you down in warmer temperatures. In general, wool fibres are durable, flexible and warm, making them suitable for a wide variety of garments. Yet, each wool-fibre variant has its own unique properties, which create differing qualities when those fibres are used in a finished item.

Cotton

Another natural fibre, frequently used for knitted garments, is cotton. This staple fibre comes from the boll that grows in the centre of the uppermost flowering section of the cotton plant. Cotton grows in warm climates, with the largest volumes of this fibre currently being grown in China and India.

The cotton fibre is noted for its strength and durability; these properties are due to the fibre's structure. The cellulose that makes up the fibre is arranged in layers that are constructed in coils, forming a spring-like shape. Fibres can vary from crop to crop, with longer staple lengths having greater strength. The cotton fibre, in contrast to wool, has a smooth surface, which results in knitwear that is made of cotton being soft and comfortable to wear. The smooth surface also provides high resistance to abrasion, making cotton a good choice for items that will be subject to intensive wear. A high level of absorbency makes it ideal for summer knitwear: the fibre pulls moisture away from the body and allows the moisture to evaporate from the fabric's surface, keeping the wearer dry.

As cotton is a natural fibre, it is often assumed to be environmentally friendly. Unfortunately, this is not the case. Cotton farming uses large amounts of pesticides and insecticides, which can cause significant harm both to workers farming the crop and to the surrounding ecosystems. Furthermore, huge quantities of water are used in production. In some areas, this has had extreme consequences; the Aral Sea, formerly one of the largest lakes in the world, has dried up as a result of its water being diverted for use in cotton farming. Various initiatives are working to promote better standards in cotton production. Organic farming aims to ensure that the workers, the soil being farmed and the ecosystems surrounding this crop remain healthy. However, there are drawbacks where organic farming is concerned, such as lower productivity and higher costs.

Silk

Silk is unique in both origin and structure, being a naturally occurring filament fibre. It has been used in knitwear for centuries, with early examples demonstrating that silk was frequently being used in combination with cotton. The fibre is spun by a

Fig. 3.4 Cotton fibres are extracted from the white fluffy balls, known as bolls, that grow at the top of cotton plants.

caterpillar – popularly known as a silkworm – in the process of making its cocoon. In the wild, the moth growing inside, when it is fully formed, breaks the cocoon open. When silk is farmed, however, the unbroken cocoon is dropped into boiling water. It can then be unwound to obtain the continuous-filament silk fibre. The inherent shine of silk, caused by the triangular cross section of the fibre and the way that light reflects off of this smooth surface, gives it a lustrous quality. Strength is another inherent property of the silk fibre, as is drape; both are due to the fibre being a continuous filament.

Other natural fibres

Natural fibres, such as bamboo, hemp and linen that are alternatives to cotton and silk, are increasingly being used for knitwear. Bamboo is a fast-growing plant that can be harvested regularly. In contrast to that of cotton, the growing of bamboo has little negative impact on the environment, with no need for the application of pesticides, and is associated with high levels of carbon dioxide absorption and oxygen production. Furthermore, bamboo can be grown by using rainwater, and, because it is cut rather than uprooted during harvesting, its production aids maintaining the integrity of the soil and sustainable soil use. Hemp has similarly positive credentials, being noted for its extremely long fibres and natural pest resistance. The farming of the flax plant, from which linen is derived, is also environmentally friendly, as it is a productive crop that uses little water and can grow without the use of pesticides. Fibres from other natural resources, such as coconut, nettle and seaweed, are also being integrated into yarns that are suitable for knitwear. Meanwhile, more unusual sources of protein can be used to produce yarns with desirable qualities; milk, for example, can be made into a protein fluid that is then spun in a similar manner to that of viscose.

Man-made fibres

Acrylic

Acrylic yarn was developed in the 1950s with the aim of mimicking the properties of wool and was soon widely used. Made from synthetic polymers, acrylic is a versatile fibre as it can be processed in many different ways. In its early stages of production, acrylic is a filament fibre; it is often later cut down to short staple lengths. Because of its low cost, acrylic is extensively used in mass-market fashion, as well as in yarns for hand knitting. It is commonly blended with wool fibres to create a yarn that takes advantage of the properties of both fibre types.

Fabrics made from acrylic typically have a soft handle, making the fibre appropriate for many types of knitwear. The fibre has a good level of crease recovery, enhancing its easy-care credentials. Colour fastness is another advantageous property; the fibre not only takes dye very effectively but also resists fading. Although acrylic is not absorbent, it will wick some moisture away from the body. However, the fibre is very prone to accumulating electrostatic energy and can feel rather plastic.

Acrylic is resistant to degradation, making it a long-lasting fibre. While this is potentially positive in terms of durability, when a garment containing a high percentage of acrylic fibre comes to the end of its useable life, it will not biodegrade. This causes significant environmental problems when we consider the extensive use of acrylic in fast-fashion ranges and the high volumes of such garments that end up in landfill.

Other synthetic fibres

Although polyester is commonly used in woven fabrics, in knitwear applications, it is typically used as a supporting fibre because of its strength, resilience and resistance to abrasion and degradation. Polyester is a filament fibre that can be blended with other fibres effectively, to create yarns with desirable properties.

First used in stockings, the nylon fibre is constructed of polymers that have a unique structure. The combination of dense areas with unstructured areas over a large surface area makes the fibre durable, strong and resistant to both creasing and abrasion; it is also highly elastic and therefore appropriate for use in underwear and sportswear. Stretch nylon is often plated with fibres, such as cotton, merino wool and viscose, to give additional stretch and recovery to the resultant fabric.

Elastomeric fibres, such as elastane, have excellent stretch and recovery properties and are important components of yarns used in contemporary knitwear. They enable the creation of form-fitting garments that hold their shape, and they can also be used to produce textiles with textural interest.

Regenerated fibres

Viscose (also known as rayon) is a different type of man-made fibre to the synthetic fibres already discussed; it is regenerated, using naturally occurring cellulose from wood pulp. Viscose was developed in the late nineteenth century with the intention of replicating the inherent properties of silk and produces a lustrous, soft fabric. Viscose is now also generated from bamboo, which is a positive development in consideration of bamboo's low environmental impact. Other regenerated fibres include modal and lyocell, which are both derived from trees. Although many dismiss these man-made fibres, mistaking them for chemically derived synthetics, these fibres have many desirable qualities and can be less environmentally harmful than is cotton.

Recycled fibres

In addition to virgin fibres that are derived from natural and synthetic materials, recycled fibres can also be used. Although interest in recycled fibres has grown in recent years, resulting from rising concerns about the environmental impact of the fashion industry, this is not a new concept. Shoddy mills have operated since the early nineteenth century, shredding waste woollen products back into fibres; these fibres can be spun into new yarn, which is often used for weaving. Today, research into

Fig. 3.5 Knitwear designer Phoebe Edwards has combined elastomeric yarns with fine merino wool to create performance fabrics for winter-sports applications that embrace the inherent properties of both fibres. PHOTOGRAPHER: RONG XUE

Fig. 3.6 Phoebe Edwards has used her high-stretch fabrics to create a full-body knitwear look. PHOTOGRAPHER: RONG XUE

recycled fibres focuses on the concept of the circular economy, where natural and man-made materials can be used time after time and kept in circulation indefinitely.

Perhaps the most widely known recycled fibre available at present is polyester that is made from plastic waste, such as used drinking bottles. This process not only repurposes waste but also reduces the use of non-renewable resources in yarn production. A diverse range of recycled yarns are available in the hand-knitting market, responding to a common desire among amateur makers to use more-sustainable materials. Despite the popularity of cotton for fashion garments, it cannot be easily recycled; the traditional shredding process reduces the fibre's staple length, affecting its quality. Another challenge for the circular economy is the use of mixed fibres in fashion textiles.

When recycled, these blends produce low-quality material that is difficult to reuse in the form of yarn. Current research is investigating the potential of innovative industrial processes to address these issues.

From fibre to yarn

Having looked into the different fibre types and their properties, we will now explore how fibres are produced, processed and turned into yarn. The nature of this overall process varies according to the type of fibre: natural or man-made, staple or filament. The process also varies according to its scale; the

Fig. 3.7 In the industrial spinning process, large carding drums rotate to separate and align the wool fibres. COURTESY: AA GLOBAL LTD

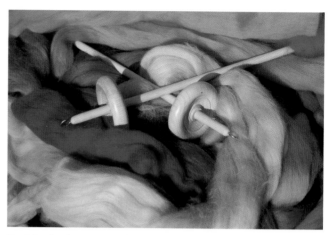

Fig. 3.8 A spinner using a drop spindle, the simplest form of hand spinning, can spin wool tops into yarn.

processing and spinning of wool, for example, can be carried out by hand by using age-old techniques or on an industrial scale. Although some specialist fibres are used in their natural undyed state, the production of yarn typically also involves dyeing. While you may not have the opportunity to see these production processes taking place in person, a good understanding of the basics will contribute to your appreciation of the yarns that you use in your design practice.

Processing of wool

Wool fibres come directly from the fleece that grows on the animal to keep it warm. In the case of sheep's wool, the fleece is removed through the process of shearing, which usually happens twice a year. This fleece is sorted, as the wool fibres from different parts of the sheep have different properties. The highest-quality fibres that are used for knitwear come from the sides and shoulders of the sheep, whereas fibres from the lower legs are often coarser and more durable, making them more suitable for use in products such as carpets and rugs. The sections of the fleece must then be processed before the fibres can be spun into yarn. The processing can be carried out in two ways, defined as woollen and worsted; these processes relate to different qualities of fibre and result in yarns with different properties. The woollen process produces an airy yarn that is softer and more insulating, while the worsted process produces a smoother and more durable yarn.

First, the fleece must be cleaned and scoured to remove any debris and dirt; it is then carded. By hand, this is done by using small, wooden hand tools called carders (or hand cards) that have small, sharp, metal bristles. Industrial carding uses the same principle, but the hand tools are replaced by large rollers. Carding teases apart the staple fibres and aligns them, producing a soft, rope-like bundle of fibres known as a sliver. The next stage is combing, where the fibres are separated by length. Woollen processing involves shorter fibres (between 2.5cm and 7.5cm, or 1in and 3in, in length) and produces a loose, web-type formation, with the fibres being positioned in multiple directions. In contrast, worsted processing selects longer fibres (over 7.5cm, or 3in, in length) and aligns them in one direction.

The final stages of the production process involve the drawing out of the sliver to produce roving (a narrower bundle of fibres) and then adding further elongation and twist through the spinning process, to produce the finished yarn. As well as reducing the strand's thickness, these processes further combine the fibres and add strength.

When fibres or yarns are twisted together to the left, this action is known as adding S twist and results in S-twist yarn; when twisted to the right, this action is known as adding Z twist and results in Z-twist yarn. Usually, when fibres are spun into yarn, a Z twist is used. The amount of twist affects the resultant yarn. High-twist yarns (those with a large number of twists per unit length of the yarn) are usually produced for use in woven fabrics; if used for knitting, these yarns can create very dense and inflexible fabrics.

Fig. 3.9 During the spinning process, bundles of fibres are drawn out and twisted, to produce finished yarns. COURTESY: AA GLOBAL LTD

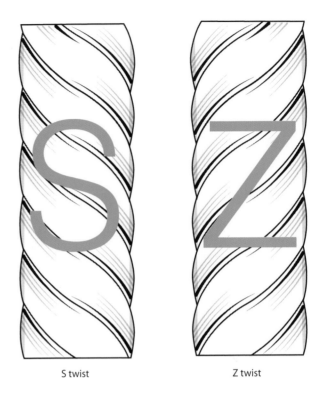

S twist   Z twist

Fig. 3.10 Look closely at the next yarn that you use. Can you identify in which direction its plies – or fibres, for a single-ply yarn – were twisted?

The single-ply yarn (also called singles yarn) that is produced by the spinning process is typically then twisted together, or plied, with an S twist. Plying adds further strength and counteracts the tendency for the single-ply yarn to twist back on itself, therefore making the plied yarn easier to work with. It also provides the opportunity to mix plies or yarns at the final stage of production.

Processing of other fibres

After a cotton crop has been harvested, either by hand or by machine, the fibres from the boll must be processed. The first stage, which dries out the raw material, is known as ginning. The dry material is then passed through cleaning machines that remove debris. Circular saws with small teeth are used to separate the cotton fibres from the seeds, before the fibres are gathered into bails and transported to a mill.

Before spinning, the cotton is treated in a similar way to that of wool, being cleaned, carded and combed to align the fibres in parallel rows, and any fibres that are too short are discarded. The slivers produced by this process are taken through drawing machines to elongate and compress the fibres. The final stage is for the roving to be spun and plied into yarn, again adding strength through elongation and the introduction of twist.

The production of man-made fibres is quite different to that of natural fibres. Both synthetic and regenerated fibres are created by the fibre-forming material being forced through holes known as spinnerets, via a process known as extrusion.

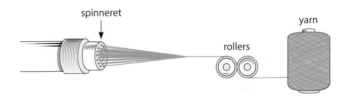

Fig. 3.11 Man-made yarns are produced by extruding the raw material through a spinneret.

When the material is extruded, a continuous-filament thread is formed. As these fibres are produced with human control operating at every stage, the fibre can be altered, depending on the properties required. This is done through texturizing, crimping and varying the cross section of the fibre, often to mimic the properties of natural fibres. Filaments can be twisted and plied together to form yarn; they can also be cut to create staple fibres. The conversion into staple fibres allows natural and synthetic fibres (such as wool and acrylic, respectively) to be blended. The fibres are combined prior to spinning, in order to ensure an even distribution of the different fibres throughout the yarn.

Fig. 3.12 This Teeswater fleece is being hand dyed at the fibre stage.

Fig. 3.13 The hand-dyeing process creates a variegated shade throughout the fibres of the dried hand-dyed fleece.

Fig. 3.14 A skein-winding machine is used to prepare yarns for dyeing. The resulting skeins – large, loosely wound hanks of yarn – are immersed in and saturated with dye that is contained in large vats.
PHOTOGRAPHER: ISABEL BROWN

Fig. 3.15 These skeins have been dyed with natural dyes.
PHOTOGRAPHER: ISABEL BROWN

Dyeing

Yarn can be dyed by using a variety of dyestuffs, depending on the fibre composition of the yarn and the required result of colouration. Historically, yarns were dyed by using naturally occurring substances such as cochineal (made from insects) and madder and indigo (made from plants). In addition to the dyestuff, a fixative known as a mordant is needed, in order to ensure that the colour is fast. The mordant is usually a chemical substance, and the type of mordant that is used will vary depending on the yarn being dyed. In today's yarn industry, the dyestuffs used are much more varied. Different fibres require different types of chemical dye, because of their differing chemical compositions. Acid dye is used for protein fibres such as wool; direct dye is used for cotton, linen and viscose; disperse dye is used for polyester and polyamides such as nylon; basic dye is used for acrylic; and reactive dye is used for cotton, linen, viscose, wool and silk.

For yarns that are made from blended fibres, the different fibres can be dyed separately prior to spinning. Alternatively, the blend can be dyed with more than one dyestuff in order to apply colour to each fibre type. Although all fibres have a good level of colour fastness if the fibres are dyed correctly, some fibres are naturally more colour fast than others. Acrylic, for example, is particularly colour fast, while cotton is more difficult to dye and the resultant colour fades relatively easily.

Fibres and yarns can be dyed by using a variety of methods. Stock dyeing involves putting loose fibres into vats of dye and applying heat; this method is most suitable for wool fibres. The other common method of dyeing fibres, known as top dyeing, involves applying dye to slivers. Dyed slivers of different shades can then be combined and spun into yarns. Both of these methods are used when soft, heathery colour effects are required.

The majority of dyeing is carried out at the yarn stage and produces solid shades. The yarn can be dyed in either skein or package form. Skein dyeing is used for soft and lofty yarns; the large, loosely wound hanks of yarn are immersed in large vats of dye. For package dyeing, the yarn is wound on to a hollow cylinder with holes in the centre that allow the dye to flow into the yarn. This process enables much larger quantities of yarn to be dyed at one time. Another method, space dyeing, involves different colours of dye being applied to different areas of the yarn, to create a variegated colour effect. Alternatively, knitwear can be dyed at the garment stage. Known as piece dyeing, this process can achieve a very even colour over the whole garment.

Unfortunately, the dyeing of both fibres and yarns has a negative impact on the environment. During the dyeing pro-cess, not all of the dyestuff adheres fully to the yarn; this results in some dye being present in the waste water. The waste is often also contaminated with other chemicals. This can have a severe impact on aquatic life and soil, and can lead to high levels of poisonous chemicals in the drinking water in areas surrounding the factories where dyeing takes place. Steps are being taken to reduce this impact, such as ensuring more effective cleaning of effluents and more efficient use of water and dyes. However, the issues remain a major challenge for the industry, in terms of sustainability.

Yarn counts and types

In order to make informed choices about yarn, you need to understand the specialist terminology that is used to describe it. This terminology includes the numerical figure that identifies the thickness, or count, of the yarn, as well as the terms that are used to describe different weights of hand-knitting yarn. You also need a good overview of the diverse types of yarn that you might use as a designer, from classic 2-ply yarns to specialist textured options.

Industrial yarn counts

The thickness of yarn is identified by using a numerical figure known as the yarn's count. There are many different systems for measuring and calculating count; today, the most widespread is the New Metric system. A New Metric (Nm) yarn count refers to the length in metres (m) of a single gram (g) of yarn. For example, 1g of a single end of a 17Nm yarn would be 17m long. The notation typically also includes a number before the count figure that indicates how many plies the yarn is composed of. For example, 2/17Nm is the count of a common lambswool yarn. This indicates that the yarn has two plies, each of which is 17m long per gram. The yarn as a whole, therefore, is 8.5m long per gram. Or, to think about it another way, if you took 17m of the yarn and weighed it, you would have 2g of yarn, because you have two ends of the yarn, which are plied together. A 4/5Nm yarn would be much thicker, with four plies, each 5m long per gram. The yarn as a whole would be 1.25m long per gram. The most important thing to understand is that, when using the New Metric system, the higher the second number, the finer the yarn. There are other count systems that work in a similar way, measuring the length per unit mass of the yarn. All are versions of the indirect system of measuring yarn count.

The other commonly used count system is the direct system. This measures the weight in relation to a fixed length of yarn. The most common count that is calculated by using this system is Tex. The count of yarn in Tex is measured as grams per 1,000m. For example, 1,000m of yarn with a 30 Tex count would weigh 30g. In contrast to the indirect system, a higher number relates to a thicker yarn, as it directly correlates to the weight of the yarn. Denier, which indicates grams per 9,000m, is another commonly used direct count system.

Hand-knitting yarn weights

In comparison with the specific measurements underpinning industrial yarn-count systems, the way in which hand-knitting yarns are described is rather vague. These yarns are mostly categorized by the number of ends of yarn that have been plied together to make the resultant yarn. Single-ply (or 1-ply) hand-knitting yarn is often very fine; when two of these yarns are twisted together, it results in a 2-ply yarn. Yarn of this fine weight would traditionally be used to hand knit a shawl. A 4-ply yarn is twice as thick again and would be used to knit garments such as sweaters and socks. Two ends of 4-ply yarn would be used to create what is known as double-knitting yarn. Thicker yarns such as aran, chunky and super chunky move away from the ply categorization and vary in terms of the number of ends.

However, if you unravel some double-knitting yarn today, you are unlikely to find eight ends of yarn. The yarn is no longer even equivalent in thickness to two ends of 4-ply yarn; the name has deviated from its original logic. Overall, the convention of referring to yarn thickness by ply is rather confusing. After all, a single ply can vary greatly in thickness; for example, a roving yarn would have only one ply, but it is very thick. A more reliable way of comparing the thickness of hand-knitting yarn is to look at the length per weight, for example, the number of metres of yarn in a 50g ball. This information is frequently included in the information on the ball band of the yarn.

Yarn types

If we put together all of the information discussed so far, it is easy to see that there are many types of yarn that you might use as a designer. Yarns might be made up of a single fibre or might be blended. Fibres can be blended before the spinning process; alternatively, yarns made from different fibres

Fig. 3.16 Fancy yarns can be used to great effect in knitwear. Surface interest can be added to the garment simply through the choice of yarn.
DESIGNER: MICHAL LESIN-DAVIS

can be plied together to create both visually and functionally interesting yarns. Yarns vary dramatically in terms of count, from ultra-fine industrial yarns to incredibly chunky options that are suitable only for hand knitting. They can also vary in terms of ply, although the standard formation, especially for machine-knitting yarns, is 2-ply yarn.

Many yarns are relatively straightforward in design, with a regular, smooth surface and no deviation in diameter or texture throughout their length. Such yarns will be used when the designer primarily wants to explore structure, colour or silhouette. In contrast, fancy yarns have interesting aesthetic features. Fancy yarns can be used to great effect in knitwear, adding surface interest to the garment. Textural fancy yarns usually combine a basic ground or core yarn and optional fine binder yarn with an effect yarn that adds aesthetic or textural

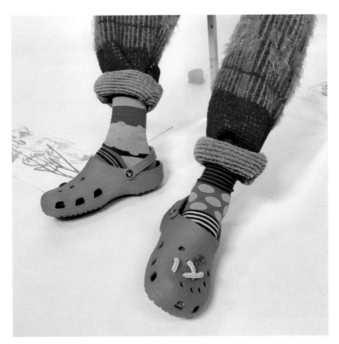

Fig. 3.17 The dynamic use of colour can enhance the impact of diverse yarns. DESIGNER: MICHAL LESIN-DAVIS

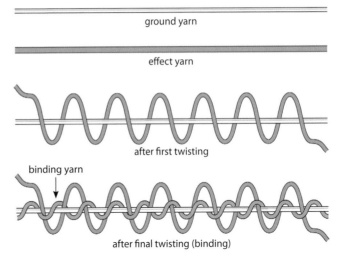

Fig. 3.18 A bouclé yarn is created through the combination of ground, effect and binder yarns. The loops are created by feeding in the yarns at different speeds during the plying process.

interest. For example, a slub yarn can be created through the addition of small amounts of roving to the effect yarn, with the basic yarn providing stability. If an effect yarn is fed in faster than the core and binder yarns during the plying process, loops will be created on the surface of the yarn; this technique can be used to produce a bouclé yarn. When knitted, both slub yarns and bouclé yarns give irregular texture to the surface of the fabric as well as add bulk in comparison with that achieved when using a regular, smooth yarn.

Some fancy yarns, such as chenille and tape yarns, are processed in a different way to standard spun yarns. Tape yarns have a flat cross section and are constructed from a very fine yarn that is knitted into a flat tube. They give a distinctive look to both the knitted stitches and the overall fabric. A very simple yarn that can be used to great aesthetic effect in knitwear is monofilament. As the name suggests, this is a single-filament synthetic yarn that is simply extruded, with no spinning or plying being undertaken, giving a very smooth and plastic appearance to the yarn. Fine monofilament yarns can produce a wearable fabric with a good handle. Lurex yarn, with a metallic surface, is another type of synthetic fancy yarn. Lurex is often plied with a complementary synthetic yarn for support. It is typically knitted in combination with other yarns to balance fabric handle with the desired aesthetic appeal.

Fig. 3.19 Monofilament and lurex yarns have been used in the striped area of this garment, to give a delicate and open feel and a lustrous surface. The chunky hand-knitted fabric creates a striking contrast in terms of scale. DESIGNER: CAT BRIERLEY

Fig. 3.20 Knitting yarns offer a wide variety of aesthetic properties. Other considerations when selecting yarn include suitability for use on a particular machine, performance in wear and attributes in terms of sustainability.

Selecting yarns

Having developed a good understanding of fibres, yarn processing and specialist terminology, you should now be in a good position to select yarn for your design project. The first challenge is to navigate the ranges on offer from the spinning industry, in order to identify suitable options. Next, you will need to weigh up various considerations, to allow you to make the right yarn choice; to strike this balance, you should refer back to your brief and your research.

Working with spinners

The spinning industry is global, with China having the largest concentration of yarn producers. This is a relatively recent shift; there were many UK and European spinners until competition from overseas companies priced them out of the market in the late 1980s and early 1990s. There are still specialist spinners operating in Europe, with luxury yarns being spun in Italy and a good number of small-scale spinners operating in the UK, often working with pure wool and specialist sheep breeds. International trade fairs are key events for many spinning companies, as this is where they present their new seasonal collections of yarns, either directly to clients or through agents.

The yarns that you knit with have all been designed. Even a simple natural cotton yarn has been carefully developed in order to sit as part of a yarn supplier's collection. Yarn design involves the consideration of properties including surface qualities, handle and colour. Spinners use trend research to inform the colour palettes and yarn designs within their collections, ensuring that the yarns that they offer are relevant for their customers and in line with future trends.

Most industrial spinners work to large minimum orders; this does not present a problem for mass-market clients who will be ordering in bulk. Large companies can even work with spinners to have bespoke shades dyed or to have their own fancy yarns developed. However, the barrier of minimum orders means that many yarn collections will not be accessible to small companies, independent knitwear designers and students. In recognition of this problem, some spinning companies offer a stock service, allowing orders as little as a single cone of yarn. Alternatively, designers working at a small scale may look for end-of-line yarns that larger companies have left over, when all of a company's knitting for the season has been completed. These yarns can be accessed via suppliers who deal in surplus yarns; such yarns are usually of good quality and reasonably priced, although the colours will not be repeatable. Details of these suppliers are provided in Websites and Further Reading.

Fig. 3.21 This outfit from a collection inspired by drag culture, by designer Emily Clark, communicates the design concept through a combination of highly decorative, textural and colourful yarns and materials. PHOTOGRAPHER: SIMON ARMSTRONG FOR NOTTINGHAM TRENT UNIVERSITY

Fig. 3.22 In this outfit, Emily Clark has used yarn as a sculptural material, for maximum impact. PHOTOGRAPHER: SIMON ARMSTRONG FOR NOTTINGHAM TRENT UNIVERSITY

Fabric aesthetics

While the first and most obvious consideration when choosing yarns may be colour, the fibre content and yarn type can also have a great effect on the resultant aesthetic of a knitted fabric. Different fibres create different effects on the surface of the knitting. Compare, for example, wool and silk: a wool yarn will produce a matt appearance that is due to the scaly surfaces of the wool fibres, whereas a yarn made from smooth and light-reflective silk fibres will give a lustrous finish. The aesthetic of a knitted fabric is also affected by its density; for machine knitting, while density is largely a result of the machine's gauge, the fibre and yarn type also have an influence. For example, if a very dense fabric is required, a yarn made from wool, with plenty of body and natural surface texture, would be the most suitable. A light and open fabric would call for a fine, smooth yarn made from a fine cotton or synthetic blend.

Textural interest can be added by using a fancy yarn, such as a bouclé, chenille or slub, or an elastomeric yarn that is used strategically in combination with other fibres. Further aesthetic effects can be achieved through the use of unconventional materials. Fine metal wires create metallic surfaces and sculptural effects in the fabric, while rubberized yarns provide a distinctive texture. Woven or jersey fabrics can be cut into strips to add surface interest. These materials can be used in machine knitting via techniques such as weaving and inlay, where the yarn does not form stitches but is integrated into the fabric. Alternatively, hand knitting allows diverse materials to be worked into the stitches of the knitting.

Technical considerations

Of course, you should not be selecting a yarn only for its aesthetic characteristics; you should also be thinking about various technical considerations. First, the yarn must be suitable for the intended machine and gauge. The general rule is that finer yarns will be used on finer-gauge knitting machines and thicker yarns (or multiple ends of fine yarns) will be used on coarser-gauge knitting machines. The accompanying table provides a general guide to yarn count and knitting-machine gauge. However, the yarn that you choose will depend on the type of fabric that you want to create. For example, you can use a fine yarn on a coarse-gauge machine to knit a looser, more open fabric. In contrast, if a stiff and solid fabric is required, you should use the thickest yarn possible to be used for that machine. The choice of yarn also depends on the structure that you are knitting; some structures require more flexible yarns and others stronger and smoother yarns, depending on the desired effect.

Another factor to consider is how the yarn performs when it is made into a garment and worn. Depending on the season and climate, you might be thinking about the yarn providing warmth or alternatively wicking away moisture from the body. The durability of the fabric should also be considered: how will the yarn that you select impact the fabric's performance over time? In addition to the general strength and durability of the yarn, you should think about issues such as pilling and yarn pulling. Pilling is much more common in yarns containing very short staple fibres, while yarns with multiple ends and slippery synthetic filaments are most susceptible to pulling.

Knitting-machine gauge	New Metric (Nm) yarn count	
	Single-ply yarn	2-ply yarn
16	32	2/64
14	24	2/48
12	16	2/32
10	13	2/26
8	10	2/20
7	8	2/16
7	5	2/10
5	4	2/8
5	3.5	2/7
3	2.5	2/5
3	2	2/4

Fig. 3.23 Table of knitting-machine gauge and typical corresponding yarn count

Fig. 3.24 With an understanding of fibres and yarn types, the knitwear designer can creatively interpret material in the sketchbook to produce appropriate samples. DESIGNER: OLIVIA LITTELL

Other factors

When working to a commercial brief, the client and market level will shape the yarn options that are available to the designer. The first consideration when designing to a specific price point is the choice of raw materials. Yarns vary widely in terms of price, from the use of luxury fibres such as cashmere and silk through to budget options such as acrylics and acrylic blends. Fluctuations in the global market of raw materials, such as cotton and wool, can influence the cost of yarns. For example, a poor cotton harvest would increase the trading price of cotton, which would then increase the spinner's price. Designers faced with challenges of price need to react and consider alternative yarn choices, to ensure that a proposed garment can be produced at a profit.

The designer should also think about the sustainability of different yarns, considering factors such as the impacts of fibre and yarn production on the environment. While some fibres are more environmentally friendly than others, as a designer, you need to be aware that there are no easy answers. Even if you have managed to source a suitable yarn that has minimal environmental impact, your garment will not automatically have impeccable sustainability credentials. There are many more factors to be considered throughout the design process, including how the garment will be constructed and, perhaps most importantly, used.

CHAPTER 4

TECHNOLOGY AND STRUCTURES

by Will Hurley

Introduction

Knitwear design is highly creative but also highly technical: you cannot design knitted fabrics or knitwear without an understanding of the knitted structure. The deeper this understanding, the more you will be able to exploit the unique characteristics of the knitting process, to generate innovative and forward-looking designs. A good knitwear designer, therefore, needs a detailed knowledge of the ways in which different knitted structures can be constructed and an appreciation of the ways in which these structures behave on the body. The designer also needs the vision to apply this knowledge creatively in relation to their design concept.

This chapter will help you to develop your understanding of the technical side of knitting, establishing basic principles and exploring the diverse range of single- and double-jersey structures that you can select from when designing. It includes an outline of the many different technologies currently in use, including flatbed knitting machines, circular machines and machines capable of knitting seamless fabric (commonly known as seamless machines), and discusses the complex computerized systems that are used to translate designs from sketch to sample in today's industry.

Weft and warp knitting

Knitwear fabric can be produced by using two distinct manufacturing technologies: weft and warp. There are inherent differences in the form of each structure and how it is achieved, meaning that a weft-knitted fabric cannot be created on a warp-knitting machine and vice versa. The main difference is the path that the yarn takes when a loop, or stitch, is formed. In weft knitting, the yarn is laid horizontally across the knitted course (row), while, in warp knitting, the yarn is laid vertically along one or more knitted wales (columns). Because of its versatility, weft knitting is the technology most commonly used in the production of knitted fashion outerwear.

This double-jersey fabric was produced by combining striped-back jacquard and tubular jacquard structures, resulting in a three-dimensional effect DESIGNER: WILL HURLEY.

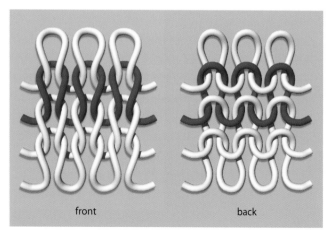

Fig. 4.1 Weft knitting is created from horizontal courses of interlocked loops. In this representation of the front of a single-jersey fabric, the stitches have the appearance of forming columns of Vs, while on the back the stitches have the appearance of forming interconnecting semicircles.
COURTESY: ADVANCED TEXTILES RESEARCH GROUP, NOTTINGHAM TRENT UNIVERSITY

Weft knitting

Weft knitting is built from horizontal courses of interlocked loops, arranged in vertical wales. The yarn travels along the course, taking an alternating, curved path. The geometry of the loops that are formed by this path gives weft-knitted fabric its inherent properties of stretch and flexibility. All hand knitting is weft-knitted, while the lineage of knitting-machine inventions described in Chapter 1, from Lee's sixteenth-century stocking frame to today's industrial flatbed machines, also produce this structure.

Weft-knitting machines can be broadly split into two categories: fabric-knitting machines and garment-panel machines. Fabric-knitting machines produce large, fixed-width lengths of fabric, much like woven fabric. The fabric produced is then cut to shape and the resultant pieces sewn together. Garment-panel machines produce garment-sized pieces; these may be rectangular garment blanks, from which the shaped garment panels must be cut and sewn, or fully fashioned (ready-shaped) garment panels. The production of fully fashioned knitwear is much more efficient in terms of raw-material use than is cut-and-sew production, because little waste is created.

Weft-knitting machines usually consist of one or more needle beds that contain needles that move within a narrow channel called a trick. As the needles move up and down sequentially across the needle bed, yarn is introduced by either a yarn carrier or a yarn feeder to facilitate the loop-forming process. Today's machines use latch or compound needles, which pick up the yarn and draw it through the stitch from the previous course.

The scale of the stitches that form weft-knitted fabrics can be varied dramatically. In hand knitting, the size of the stitch is affected by the size of the needle; in machine knitting, the most influential factor is the gauge of the machine. Gauge is usually measured as the number of needles per inch within the needle bed. When many needles are present per inch, small stitches and a fine-gauge fabric are produced; conversely, when few needles are present per inch, large stitches and a coarse-gauge fabric are produced. The size of the stitch is also controlled by the tension at which the yarn is delivered to the needles and how far the needle pulls the yarn through the stitch from the previous course. The gauge of machine has a direct impact upon the length of time required for manufacture: to produce a given length of fabric, machines of finer gauges are required to produce more knitted courses than are required to be produced by a coarser-gauge machine. This increases manufacturing costs, although the cost can often be offset by a reduction in yarn consumption.

Warp knitting

Warp knitting is an entirely different type of construction to that of weft knitting. Because in warp knitting the yarn runs vertically up the wales, a separate feed of yarn is needed for every working needle. Although there are differences between the mechanics of the two main classifications of warp technology, tricot and raschel, the fundamental principles are the same. The needles ascend and descend in one motion, with yarn guide bars facilitating the movement of yarn from needle to needle. This movement can be controlled to create a range of structures; its efficiency makes warp knitting the fastest method of fabric manufacture.

While warp knitting is widely used for technical textiles, it also has fashion knitwear applications. Many of Missoni's distinctive high-fashion knits are warp-knitted; the technology is also used to produce knitted-lace fabric. In recent years, seamless warp-knitted garments have been developed, such as base-layer and sportswear items. This production method is not without waste, particularly around the point where the sleeve and body connect and between the end of one garment and the start of the next. An iconic example of seamless warp knitting is Issey Miyake's A-POC range, launched in 1997. These customizable garments, engineered from tubes of raschel fabric, exploit the fact that warp-knitted fabric does not ladder when cut.

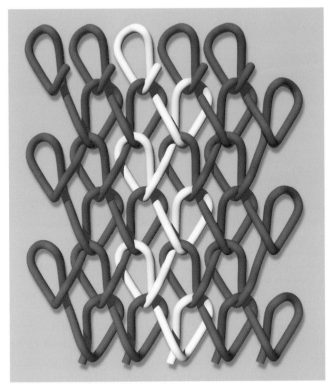

Fig. 4.2 In warp knitting, the yarn runs vertically up the wale, with a separate feed of yarn being required for each working needle.
COURTESY: ADVANCED TEXTILES RESEARCH GROUP, NOTTINGHAM TRENT UNIVERSITY

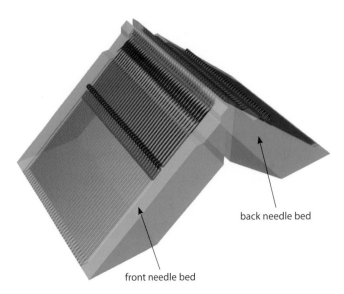

back needle bed

front needle bed

Fig. 4.3 Flatbed knitting machines typically have two needle beds that are arranged in an inverted-V formation. COURTESY: ADVANCED TEXTILES RESEARCH GROUP, NOTTINGHAM TRENT UNIVERSITY

Fig. 4.4 When knitting a double-jersey fabric on an industrial flatbed knitting machine, the yarn alternates between the needles on each bed.
COURTESY: ADVANCED TEXTILES RESEARCH GROUP, NOTTINGHAM TRENT UNIVERSITY

Weft-knitting technologies

Today, weft knitting can be produced on a range of distinct knitting-machine platforms: flatbed machines, seamless machines, knitting frames, circular machines and machines capable of knitting purl fabric (commonly known as purl machines). Although basic in comparison, the needles that are used to produce hand knitting can be regarded as another type of knitting technology.

Flatbed machines

Flatbed machines are the most varied category of weft-knitting machines and range from hand-operated domestic machines to advanced automated machines that use the latest technology. While being knitted by the machine, the shape of the panel can be varied by decreasing or increasing the number of stitches being worked; this means that fully fashioned garment panels can be produced. The maximum width of the panel is limited by the length of the machine's needle bed.

Industrial flatbed machines, also known as V-bed machines, typically have two beds that are aligned in an inverted-V configuration. The beds can knit either independently, to create single-jersey fabrics, or together, to create double-jersey fabrics;

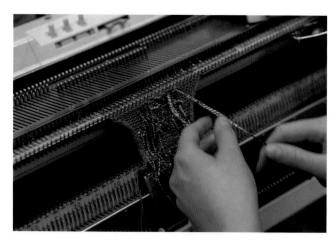

Fig. 4.5 This single-bed domestic knitting machine is being used to knit a sample that involves the application of the weaving technique. The rib attachment, with a vertical bed of needles, is attached to the machine but not in use.

Fig. 4.6 Seamless flatbed knitting machines knit a garment in one operation, without the need for seaming. The tubular sleeves and body of the cardigan on this Shima Seiki Wholegarment machine are being knitted side by side.

striping, jacquard and intarsia patterns can be created through the use of multiple yarn carriers. Programmed by using CAD/CAM systems, industrial flatbed machines are capable of producing diverse outputs, from fashion knitwear garments to innovative sports shoes and various types of technical textiles. Industrial flatbed machines range from 3 gauge to 21 gauge, with the coarser gauges generally being more prevalent. While industrial flatbed machines are incredibly versatile, the cost of this versatility is speed; flatbed machines are the slowest in terms of industrial fabric production. Yet, they are efficient in terms of space, and sample panels can be produced easily in comparison with their production by other industrial machines.

Hand-powered flatbed (or hand-flat) machines, such as Dubied machines, operate according to the same effective principles as do industrial flatbed machines. Again, they have two beds that are positioned in an inverted-V configuration and range in gauge from 2.5 gauge to 14 gauge. Domestic knitting machines typically have just one bed of needles, although rib attachments can be used to produce double-jersey fabrics. Many have built-in patterning mechanisms. The standard domestic machine is 7 gauge; coarser- and finer-gauge versions are available, though much less common.

Seamless machines

Seamless flatbed machines can knit a fully completed seamless garment in one operation, without the need for garment make-up. To do so, multiple tubes are produced simultaneously,

side by side. For example, the body and sleeves of a sweater are knitted as three separate tubes until they need to be connected at the underarm point; they are then joined to form a single tube. The single tube will then progressively be reduced in width, to mimic the meeting of the sleeve heads with the garment body that would occur in the production of a seamed garment.

There are two distinct ways in which seamless flatbed machines can be configured. The conventional formation of two beds can be used, with alternate needles working on each bed and the empty needles facilitating the movement of stitches. Alternatively, two extra knitting beds can be added to create an X-bed machine, for the production of finer-gauge garments. The main flatbed seamless platforms are Wholegarment (by Japanese manufacturer Shima Seiki) and Knit and Wear (by German manufacturer Stoll).

Knitting frames

The category of knitting frames includes both the original hand frame invented by William Lee in 1589 and the straight-bar frames developed by William Cotton and other machine manufacturers almost three centuries later. The surviving Lee hand frames are largely preserved in museum collections, with a few notable exceptions still being used for production. Although the straight-bar frame has generally been superseded by the development of modern electronic flatbed knitting technology, it continues to be used to produce fully fashioned knitwear by

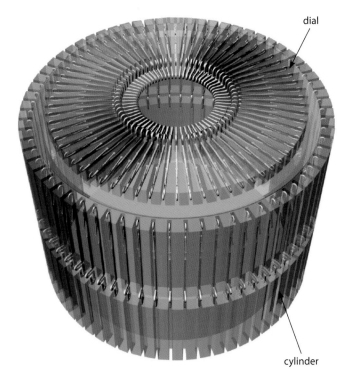

dial

cylinder

Fig. 4.7 Circular knitting machines with two needle beds create tubular fabrics with double-jersey structures. COURTESY: ADVANCED TEXTILES RESEARCH GROUP, NOTTINGHAM TRENT UNIVERSITY

heritage manufacturers such as John Smedley Ltd. Unlike both flatbed and circular knitting machines, the gauge of a straight-bar frame is expressed over 1½ inches. Therefore, a 21 gauge straight-bar frame equates to a 14 gauge flat or circular knitting machine. The straight-bar frame is a long multi-sectional machine, with each section producing duplicate knitted panels. While there are some rib frames in existence, the most common version produces single-jersey fabric.

Circular machines

The category of circular machines corresponds to a broad range of machines in which a machine's bed is arranged in a cylinder and that is therefore capable of producing tubular fabric. A single cylindrical bed produces single jersey; in some cases, a secondary bed called a dial is positioned on top of the cylinder to allow the production of double-jersey fabrics such as rib or jacquard. Although circular-knitting technology can produce most weft-knitted structures, the machines tend to be specialized for one particular fabric type.

Because the needles are arranged in a cylinder of a fixed size, the tubular knitted fabric is created with a fixed diameter. Circular machines are therefore produced in different diameters, depending on their intended use, for producing a broad range of fabrics – from hosiery to large-scale fabric production. Italian manufacturer Santoni has developed a range of machines specifically for applications including the production of underwear, outerwear, swimwear and sportswear. Garment tubes can be knitted with fabric of a very fine quality, of up to 40 gauge, and produced at high speeds. While this technology is marketed as producing knitting that is seamless, it might be more pertinent to refer to it as producing knitting with fewer seams, given that a degree of sewing construction is typically required to complete the garments.

Purl machines

Purl knitting, sometimes referred to as links-links knitting, occurs when both knit (face) and purl (reverse) stitches are visible on one side of the fabric. Purl or links-links machines have two horizontal beds that are positioned directly opposite each other, arranged in either a circular or a flatbed configuration. A single needle with a hook and latch on each end travels between both beds; depending on where it is positioned, the needle will knit either a knit or a purl stitch. While flatbed purl machines have been largely replaced by electronic flatbed knitting-machine technology, circular purl machines continue to be produced.

Hand knitting

Hand knitting, which predates all forms of machine knitting, creates the same weft-knitted structure as do all of the technologies discussed so far. It is much slower to produce and therefore commercial hand knitting is generally restricted to areas of the world in which labour costs are relatively low. As a hobby, however, hand knitting is enjoying a period of resurgence, and, consequently, there are opportunities for designers to produce innovative hand-knitting patterns for use by skilled hobbyists. The related craft of crochet, while often categorized with hand knitting, creates a very different structure.

Hand knitting can be produced at a wide range of gauges; with the use of thick needles and yarn, fabrics can be produced that are far chunkier than those fabrics knitted on machines of the coarsest gauges. Hand-knitted items are invariably knitted to shape, either as separate garment panels (typically knitted

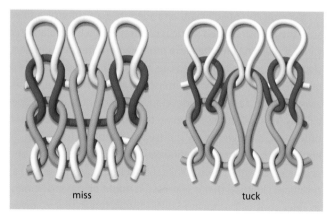

Fig. 4.8   Every weft-knitted fabric is built up from three basic stitch elements: knit, miss and tuck. COURTESY: ADVANCED TEXTILES RESEARCH GROUP, NOTTINGHAM TRENT UNIVERSITY

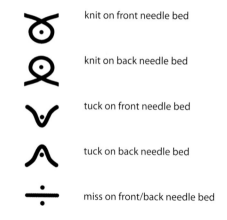

Fig. 4.9   The stitch elements can be represented by using symbols on a stitch diagram, to communicate how a particular structure is created.

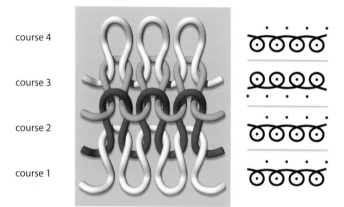

Fig. 4.10   Stitch diagrams are built from the bottom up, as the corresponding stitches would be when being knitted. This example represents a purl structure, which combines knit (face) stitches and purl (reverse) stitches on the front of the knitted fabric. COURTESY: ADVANCED TEXTILES RESEARCH GROUP, NOTTINGHAM TRENT UNIVERSITY

Weft-knitted structures

Having looked at the various technologies that are available for producing weft-knitted fabrics, we can now look at the weft-knitted structures in more detail. In this section, we will establish some key principles, examining the basic stitch elements, the single- and double-jersey structures and the process of shaping.

Knit, miss and tuck stitch elements

It is amazing to think that, despite the endless diversity of weft-knitted structures, all are constructed by using a combination of three basic stitch elements: knit, miss and tuck.

- Knit: the yarn is picked up by the needle and pulled through the stitch of the previous course to form a new stitch.
- Miss (or slip): the yarn travels past the stitch of the previous course, creating a float.
- Tuck: the yarn is picked up by the needle for the yarn to sit alongside the stitch of the previous course.

on two needles) or as tubular, seamless pieces (typically knitted on a circular needle or a set of double-ended needles). Many of the machine-knitted structures described in this chapter can be created via hand knitting; some procedures, such as decreasing many times across a single course, are much more easily achieved by hand than on a machine.

Single- and double-jersey structures

Weft-knitted structures can be subdivided into two categories of fabrics: those knitted on a single set of needles (single-jersey or single-bed fabrics) and those created by using two sets of needles (double-jersey or double-bed fabrics). Many variations can be knitted within each category, as will be explored later in the chapter. First, we will discuss the fundamentals of each one.

In single jersey, all of the stitches are configured in the same way. On the front of the fabric, you see the knit side, or face, of each stitch, with the stitches having the appearance of being arranged as columns of Vs. On the back of the fabric, you see the purl side, or reverse, of each stitch, with the stitches having the appearance of being arranged as interconnecting semicircles. If you look at the knitwear in your wardrobe, it is likely that the majority of the pieces will have been created by using a single-jersey structure. Why? First, single jersey is more economical to produce in terms of yarn usage, and therefore cost, by using only around 50–60 per cent of the yarn that is required for the production of a double-jersey fabric of a similar visual effect. Second, single jersey is often preferable in terms of fabric quality; the fabric is relatively light and, therefore, the garment will not stretch under its own weight. Third, this structure is easier to knit to shape than are double-jersey structures. Finally, single jersey provides a suitable base structure for colourwork techniques such as striping, intarsia and Fair Isle. It should be noted that single jersey has a tendency to roll along its edges. This is an inherent feature of the structure and can be resolved during garment manufacture.

When a secondary needle bed is available for the creation of double-jersey fabric, it is possible to produce a wider range of knit structures. The secondary bed is fundamental for the creation of rib structures, which are widely used for cuffs and welts. Double-jersey fabric does not curl at the edges and has greater extensibility than does single jersey, as a result of the movement of yarn between the two beds. On flatbed machines, the two beds can be used to produce a tube of single-jersey fabric or to insert small tubular sections within a double-jersey structure, by knitting on each bed alternately. Using the inlay technique, yarns and other materials can be incorporated into these tubular sections.

Fig. 4.11 This sweater is made from single-jersey fabric in a coarse gauge, with a 2×2 rib welt. Lace holes are used for decoration and as buttonholes; the integral pocket was made by using the partial-knitting technique. DESIGNER: AMY TWIGGER HOLROYD. PHOTOGRAPHER: MEG KERR

Shaping

Flatbed knitting is unique among industrial fabric-manufacturing processes for the ability to shape: to decrease or increase the width of the fabric as it is produced. Fashioning is the term used when the fabric width is decreased; to work the fashioning, the edge stitches are moved on to adjacent needles towards the centre of the fabric panel. This movement can be of either the very edge stitch or a group of stitches.

When a group of stitches is moved to create a decrease, a fashioning mark is created; this is most often seen at the armholes and sleeve heads of a fully fashioned sweater. Fashionings can vary in terms of the number of stitches that are moved and the pitch of the transfer – that is, the number of stitch positions by which they move. This is usually one, two or three positions, with a three-position movement creating the most pronounced fashioning mark. A 2-pitch, 10-needle fashioning would see a group of ten stitches being moved in by two positions, reducing the width of the panel by two stitches. It is important to space out fashionings evenly; in general, you would knit at least the same number of courses between fashionings as the pitch of the transfer.

Widening is the term used when the fabric width is increased. This is most commonly seen on sleeves and is typically achieved by introducing a single adjacent needle at the edge of the fabric. An increase in width can also be achieved by moving groups of stitches, but this increases the cost of garment manufacture, as more time is required to knit the garment panel.

Fig. 4.12 Fashioning marks, as seen here at the armhole of a set-in-sleeve sweater, are created when stitches are moved towards the centre of a fabric panel to decrease its width. These are 3-pitch, 7-needle fashionings, spaced eight courses apart.

Binding off (casting off) is an alternative shaping process that is used when a horizontal finished edge is required, such as the base of the armhole and the centre of a round neckline. It can also be used to generate a decrease that is too shallow to be achieved via fashioning, such as for a shoulder slope. One or two stitches are knitted and moved to adjacent needles, with the process being repeated until the stitches of the relevant section of knitting have been cleared from the needles.

Single-jersey structures

In this section, we will explore a range of fabrics that can be knitted on a single needle bed. Some techniques have more than one name; these are indicated in brackets. It should be noted that many of these processes, while most commonly used for the production of single-jersey fabrics, are also applicable to double-jersey structures.

Striping

Striping is the simplest method of combining colours in a knitted fabric. It is also an excellent technique for combining different thicknesses of yarn. Depending on the number of yarn carriers available, a range of effects can be created, from simple two-colour stripes to much more complex colour layouts. Many of the techniques described in the following sections can be carried out in conjunction with striping, in order to add texture and/or distort the linear appearance of the block colour.

Fig. 4.13 Fair Isle fabrics are knitted by using two colours in each course of a single-jersey structure. This design by freelance designer Becky Baker had been drawn as a graph before being knitted by hand.

Fair Isle (float jacquard)

Strictly speaking, the term Fair Isle refers to the traditional hand-knitting technique, originating on the remote Scottish island of the same name, for incorporating multiple colours into knitted fabric. This distinctive technique has its own signature library of small-scale repeat patterns, which are created by knitting with two yarns in each course. However, it is now commonly used to refer to any hand- or machine-knitted single-jersey fabric that is created by using this principle.

When being knitted on a machine, a Fair Isle structure is created by selecting a repeating pattern of needles to knit the first yarn; the second yarn, usually of a different colour, follows and is knitted by only the needles that the first yarn missed. Horizontal floats are created on the reverse of the fabric wherever one of the yarns misses one or more needles. When designing a Fair Isle pattern, the length of the floats is a major consideration. Floats that are too long cause problems both during the knitting process and during wear, as there is a tendency for the floats to be snagged. As a rough guide, a yarn should never float over more needles than the gauge of the machine that is being used to knit the fabric; for example, floats should be a maximum of five needles wide on a 5 gauge machine. Because of this limitation, Fair Isle patterns tend to be small

Fig. 4.14 The intarsia technique is used to create large-scale, graphic, multi-coloured patterns, as demonstrated in this design by Genevieve Sweeney. A separate feed of yarn is required for every field of colour.

Fig. 4.15 This plated fabric has been knitted with two yarns, which swapped positions several times during the knitted course, to create the graphic pattern. DESIGNER: SOPHIE CUI

geometric or figurative representations, banded in sections along the length of the garment. If a longer float is required, a tuck stitch can be used to break up the float's horizontal length; this is referred to as accordion Fair Isle. While the Fair Isle technique usually includes only two colours within each course, different colour combinations can be used in different courses in order to increase the number of colours in the overall pattern.

Intarsia

Intarsia is another technique for knitting with multiple colours, typically being used to create large-scale geometric patterns. The most familiar application of the technique is the classic diamond-shaped argyle pattern that is commonly seen on golf sweaters. In contrast to Fair Isle knitting, where both yarns are knitted across the full width of the fabric, in intarsia, each yarn is confined to its own field or section of colour. The number of fields is limited only by the number of yarn carriers available; the latest machines have up to forty carriers. Fields must be joined together during the knitting process, usually by working tuck stitches, as, otherwise, the sections of different colours of knitting will not be connected, resulting in holes in the fabric. The group of needles on which each field is knitted can be altered for each course to create diagonal or more fluid lines, although care must be taken to avoid the formation of long floats when knitting irregular shapes.

Plating

A plated structure consists of two yarns, with a ground yarn appearing on the front of the fabric and a plated yarn on the back. A special yarn carrier introduces the plating yarn to the needle hook just after the ground yarn, placing it at the back

Fig. 4.16   This design by Keep & Share is created from two rectangles of a tuck-lace fabric, knitted in naturally coloured cashmere yarn and gathered on to a simple integral trim. PHOTOGRAPHER: MEG KERR

Fig. 4.17   This miss-stitch structure is combined with striping to create a patterned and textured fabric. DESIGNER: WILL HURLEY

of each stitch. While it is difficult to achieve perfect plating with one yarn completely hiding the other, interesting effects can be created through the combination of different yarn colours and weights. The recent development of direct-feed, belt-driven industrial machines offers the ability to swap the ground and plated yarns multiple times during the working of a knitted course. This has great potential for creating graphic patterns with an almost print-like quality.

Tuck patterning (guilloche)

Tuck patterning uses tuck stitches (or tucks) in combination with knit stitches to create textured fabrics, typically with a waffle-like structure and bulky handle. The same needle can tuck for multiple courses, to create a more pronounced effect, but there is a limit to how many tucks can be built up before the needle must knit. This is usually a maximum of six courses, though this could vary according to the thickness, elasticity and strength of the yarn. Further patterning variations can be knitted by leaving specific needles out of action, creating a ladder on either side of a tuck stitch. The combination of ladders and tucks produces an open fabric with a lace-like appearance that is quick and easy to knit in comparison with the production of true lace fabric.

Tuck patterning can also be used to weave a coarser yarn into the knitted fabric. This yarn does not form stitches but rather is laid into the needle hooks in a predetermined pattern of tucks and floats. When the main yarn is knitted for the next course, the woven yarn is locked into the fabric via the tuck stitches. As with Fair Isle, the maximum recommended length of a float is determined by the gauge of the machine. Yarns that would normally be too thick, thin or textured for the gauge of machine in use can be successfully incorporated into the fabric by using this method.

Miss stitch (slip, float or held stitch)

Just like tucks, miss stitches (or misses) – where the yarn floats past one or more needles – can be arranged to create a repeating textural pattern. Again, there is a limit to how long the same needle can be missed by the yarn, as, otherwise, if this limit is exceeded, the stitch held on the needle is likely to break. The length of the float must also be taken into consideration. This technique has many similarities to the Fair Isle technique and is often used in combination with striping to create coloured geometric patterns.

Lace

Lace structures are created by moving a stitch on to an adjacent needle. During the working of the next knitted course, the empty needle picks up the yarn, creating a hole. These decorative lace holes can be arranged to create highly complex patterns. The direction of transfer, to either the adjacent needle to the left or that to the right, is critical for the creation of the pattern, as this deflection creates a flow of movement of the fabric's stitches. Working machine-knitted lace is time-consuming, requiring in many instances thousands of stitch transfers. Transfers usually occur every two courses in order to increase productivity and reduce the possibility of dropped stitches laddering the fabric. Single-jersey lace can be created manually on a single-bed domestic machine by physically lifting and moving the stitches. Alternatively, a lace carriage could be used. When knitting on industrial machines, a second bed is required to facilitate the performance of stitch movements.

Partial knitting (gore, flechage or short-row knitting)

For partial knitting on a machine, one group of needles knits stitches as normal, while the stitches on other needles are held. This means that the knitting grows unevenly in length. Using this technique, you can knit geometric blocks of different yarns, distort the wale orientation of the fabric or create three-dimensional shapes within the structure of the knitted textile. The most common example of this three-dimensional shaping is the heel in your knitted socks; to create this shape, needles on both sides of the fabric panel are progressively put on hold and then progressively put back into action. Every two courses, at least one needle must be added or removed from the group

of needles that are knitting. Changing the number of needles that are added or removed each time will change the angle of the three-dimensional shape that is created. If the same process is used but with needles being held at only one side, a wedge shape is created; multiple wedges can be built up to produce curved, flared or frilled shapes. If the groups of needles in the hold position remain static, with no further needles being added or removed, a loop or flap of knitting will be created.

Double-jersey structures

When two needle beds are used for knitting, the structural possibilities multiply. In this section, we will explore the key categories of double-jersey fabrics, again including the alternative names that may be used for these structures.

Rib structures

When rib fabrics are knitted, the yarn alternates between being worked by needles on each bed. The concertina-like structure that is created gives rib fabrics a higher degree of extension and recoverability than that of other structures. This makes them ideal for close-fitting garments as well as the cuffs and welts that typically form the bottom of sleeve and garment panels. Many rib structures have an identical appearance on both sides of the fabric.

Rib fabrics are usually defined by the number of needles knitting on the front bed and the number of needles knitting on the back bed for one repeat of the rib pattern. A 3×3 rib would consist of three stitches being knitted on the front bed, alternating with three stitches being knitted on the back bed, while a 5×3 rib would have five stitches being knitted on the front bed and three on the back bed, alternately. Needles on each bed must be left out of action in order to facilitate the knitting of each arrangement of rib stitches.

In some cases, the same basic rib can be set out with differing numbers of needles out of action; this affects the rib fabric's appearance and performance. For example, a 1×1 rib can be created either on every needle (known as 1×1 all-needle rib) or on every other needle on each bed (known as 1×1 half-gauge rib). A rib pattern with a repeat of two stitches being worked on the front bed and two stitches being worked on the back bed can be set up with either two needles out of action in between the working needles or just one needle out of action. In this case, the rib is named according to the needles in and

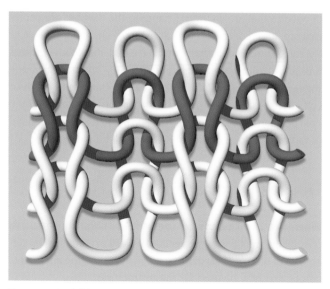

Fig. 4.18 In rib fabrics, the yarn alternates between needles on each bed, to create an extensible concertina-like structure. COURTESY: ADVANCED TEXTILES RESEARCH GROUP, NOTTINGHAM TRENT UNIVERSITY

1×1 all needle rib

1×1 half gauge rib

2×1 rib

2×2 rib

Fig. 4.19 As these stitch diagrams indicate, basic ribs can be set out in different ways, to create fabrics with varying characteristics.

Fig. 4.20 This relaxed-style garment by designer Charlotte Cameron was knitted in full-cardigan stitch with two yarns: a blended yarn of British Bluefaced Leicester and Masham wools, and a Donegal-tweed yarn made of lambswool and mulberry silk. PHOTOGRAPHER: CALLUM BAIGRIE

out of action, and, therefore, the two varieties are known, rather confusingly, as 2×2 rib and 2×1 rib.

A machine-knitted mock rib has the visual appearance of a traditional rib layout, but it is achieved by combining sections of 1×1 all-needle rib and single jersey. It has a very stable structure that does not contract as much as does a true rib fabric.

Cardigan (fisherman's rib, brioche) and milano structures

Cardigan structures are created when tucks are incorporated into a rib structure; this increases the bulkiness of the fabric.

For half cardigan fabric, stitches are knitted on the front bed whereas tucks are formed on the back bed, followed by a course of knitting on both beds. This means that there are twice as many loops on the front side of the fabric compared to the number on the back, creating a denser knitted fabric. Cardigan (also known as full cardigan) fabric is a more balanced fabric, produced by knitting on the front bed and tucking on the back bed in one direction, and tucking on the front bed and knitting on the back bed in the other direction. Racking – shifting the position of the back needle bed in relation to the front needle bed – can be used while knitting cardigan stitches, to distort the fabric's structure and create a zigzag structural effect.

Milano fabrics result when the fabric properties of single and double jersey are combined. Half milano fabric is created when one course of 1×1 rib is worked, followed by one course of knitting only on the back bed. Milano (also known as full milano) fabric results when a course that is knitted only on the front bed is added to this sequence. These fabrics have the density of double jersey but very little extension, as a result of the single-jersey component of the structure, creating a fabric that is most often used to mimic the behaviour of a woven material.

Double-jersey jacquard structures

A knitted jacquard fabric is created when the yarns of two or more yarn carriers that are holding different-coloured yarns are selectively knitted across the width of the fabric to create a pattern. The floats at the back of the fabric limit the size of each field of colour when knitting Fair Isle fabric, meaning that patterns must be small in scale. To overcome this limitation, double-jersey structures are required. Rather than creating floats, these structures are created when the colours not needed for the pattern are knitted on the back bed. Much more complex patterns can be created; the finer the gauge of the machine, the higher the resolution of the design that is achievable to knit. With the use of CAD/CAM technology, patterns need not be limited to a set repeat. More colours can be used in each course, although this has a direct bearing on the weight and density of the fabric.

There are several different double-jersey jacquard structures. In a striped-back jacquard, the yarns of colours not in use on the front bed (which creates the pattern side of the fabric) are knitted on every needle on the back bed. This gives a striped appearance on the reverse of the fabric. The more yarn colours that are used, the more that the stitches on the front of the jacquard fabric will be stretched. For example, in a five-colour striped-back jacquard, there are four courses that are knitted on the back bed for every one course that is knitted on the front bed. This stretching can be addressed through the working of a bird's-eye jacquard structure. In this case, each colour of yarn is knitted on only every second needle on the back bed when that yarn is not being used on the pattern side of the fabric, therefore halving the number of courses on the back of the fabric.

Another variation, tubular jacquard, usually consists of just

Fig. 4.21   For this bird's-eye jacquard fabric, the yarn not in use on the front of the fabric was knitted on every second needle on the back needle bed. DESIGNER: JANE TAYLOR

two colours of yarn and is notable for creating the same pattern on both sides of the fabric. The first yarn colour is knitted on the front bed while the second yarn colour is knitted on the back bed. Whenever a change of colour is required in the pattern, the yarn colours swap to the opposite bed. To reduce the weight of the fabric and therefore the amount of yarn required, a ladder-back jacquard structure can be used as an alternative. This reduces the number of needles knitting on the back bed of the double-jersey jacquard, creating the appearance of ladders. For example, a 4×1 ladder-back would have four needles out of action and one needle in action on the back bed. This type of jacquard is often combined with intarsia, to create more complex patterns.

Purl fabrics (links-links or knit-purl fabrics)

Purl fabrics include patterns that are created by using combinations of knit, or face, stitches (with the appearance of Vs) and purl, or reverse, stitches (with the appearance of semicircles) on the front of the knitted fabric. Requiring the movement of stitches between beds, this principle can be used to knit a range of patterns such as basket weave, moss stitch and garter stitch. The purl stitches tend to stand proud of the knit stitches, creating a three-dimensional effect. These patterns are traditionally seen on fishermen's ganseys. When combined with plating, two-colour structural patterns can be achieved.

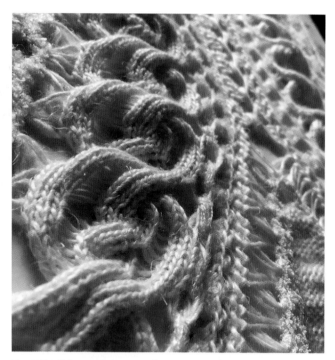

Fig. 4.22 This swatch mixes machine-knitted cables and ladders with open crochet techniques. DESIGNER: JO BEE

Cables and Aran knitting

Cables consist of instances of two or more adjacent knit or purl stitches swapping positions over multiple courses, to create a twisted or interlaced effect that is reminiscent of Celtic knotwork. Often combined with purl patterns, cables usually consist of paired groups of stitches being moved and can have multiple pairs swapping positions, to create highly complex patterns. Cables are defined by the number of stitches swapping positions and the direction of the twist. The cable pairs do not need to be of equal numbers of stitches, with some interesting effects being created by the movement of uneven pairs of stitches. For machine knitting, cables usually never exceed a group of 3×3 stitches being moved, as larger stitch movements can cause breakages of the yarn. However, the appearance of much larger cables can be achieved by combining multiple smaller cables in a defined pattern. A related technique, a component of Aran knitting, involves the movement of knit (face) stitches over an area of purl (reverse) stitches, to create a travelling cord.

Design translation

Designers working in a small-studio context will often knit their own fabrics, moving flexibly between machine, mannequin and sketchbook, in order to explore and develop ideas. In industry, sophisticated computerized programming systems will typically be used in order to realize designs.

Programming industrial machines

Of all knitting technologies, the modern electronic flatbed machine, with its extensive patterning and shaping capabilities, is unique in terms of the range of structures and shapes that it can produce. This versatility has been maximized by the development of CAD/CAM programmes, which have automated the control of stitch, colour and shape patterning and thereby enabled complete control of the knitted product.

CAD/CAM systems are proprietary to each machine manufacturer; there is no common programming language shared between platforms. However, the systems typically use a graphical interface, with each stitch being represented by either an icon or a colour relating to a specific function. Programming using these systems is a highly skilled and technical process, typically carried out by specialist technicians or design technologists.

Recognizing that a more intuitive programming platform would enable designers to work more directly with industrial technology, Shima Seiki has developed a virtual knitting-design programme, SDS-ONE APEX3. This interface allows for the realistic digital development of knitted fabrics, garment silhouettes and colourways. The system generates the technical knitting code in parallel to the virtual sample, which can then be optimized by a knitwear technician for production.

Sampling in industry

In some industrial contexts, samples will be produced by a manufacturer on the basis of instructions that are put together by the designer and are included within a tech pack; this approach is discussed in Chapters 6 and 7. In other contexts, sampling involves a much more direct collaboration between the designer and the knitwear technician. This relationship should be viewed as a creative partnership, with the designer drawing upon the expertise of the technician to achieve the designer's creative vision. The technician's experience is critical

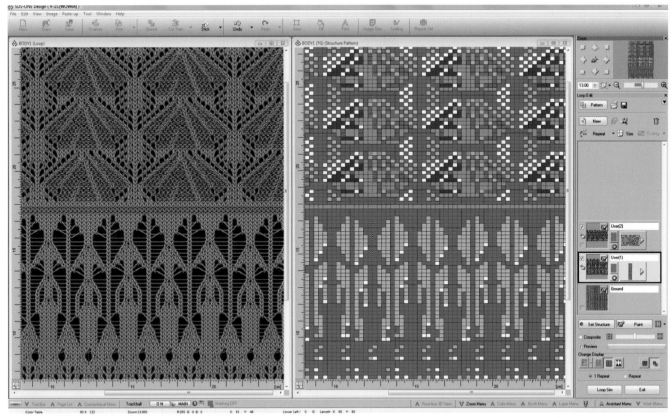

Fig. 4.23 Shima Seiki's SDS-ONE APEX3 knitting-design programme enables the visualization of a virtual sample alongside the technical knitting code. This complex lace structure is created through the arrangement of decorative holes.

to achieve a design that is technically possible and meets the production criteria. The iterative process of fabric and garment development showcases the designer's ability to work within a set of constraints to deliver a creative outcome and also the technician's ability to push the technology.

The collaborative sampling process usually commences with the designer generating a sample request, which includes all of the information this is needed to create a specific knitted structure with a particular yarn on a defined gauge of machine. The designer and the technician will discuss the design requirements and, depending on their complexity, may investigate alternative methods to achieve the desired effect. The technician may choose to adapt existing programmes; many manufacturers have a library of designs, in some instances developed over many years, and these designs can continually be revisited and reinterpreted. The machine manufacturers Shima Seiki and Stoll both provide online shops where CAD/CAM programmes can be purchased.

Once a CAD/CAM programme has been generated and inputted to the machine, a series of quality swatches are produced to identify an appropriate stitch density for the samples. These swatches will then undergo the same finishing processes, such as wet finishing and steaming, as intended for the final garment, in order to assess fabric quality and stitch density after such treatment. Identifying the correct stitch size is critical; many production issues can be traced to knitting either too tight or too slack on the machine. Factors such as knitting times and yarn consumption must be recorded, in order to allow an accurate costing to be calculated. This costing process will be ongoing during sampling and will be used to inform the designer of any amendments that are needed to meet the target price.

CHAPTER 5

DESIGN AND COMMUNICATION

by Jane Thomson

Introduction

This chapter focuses on the core activity of the knitwear designer: generating original fabric and garment ideas, and refining them into finished designs. This process is initiated by creatively responding to the research that has been gathered. The designer must then use their understanding of fibres, yarn, technology and structures to produce initial fabric samples and refine them into a coherent collection of textile designs. Alongside this process, garment ideas are explored, developed and finalized, to produce a balanced and desirable range that meets the needs of the project brief.

The design process is highly personal; there is no set way to work. Every designer will respond to their research throughout the design process in different ways. Drawing is a valuable skill for designers that enables the exploration and communication of fabric designs and garment designs. Alternative methods can also be used, including CAD, collage and working in three dimensions. These diverse approaches are applicable both to the development of ideas and to the presentation of the finished collection.

Responding to research

The design process begins with, and depends on, research. As discussed in Chapter 2, at the start of a project, you need to undertake primary and secondary research. If working for a high street retailer, research may begin by undertaking the production of a shop report, to understand the market level, or by using information from a forecasting company, to understand appropriate trends. In other projects, the gathering of personal inspiration may be the most important element of the research process. The research will then be developed into an original design concept, to be used when generating your own design ideas. The concept will influence the choice of yarn and colour palette, the design of the fabric and garment, and the presentation of the collection.

Design research is visually communicated through a design-generation board. The board communicates the designer's ideas with sketches, photographs and annotation. DESIGNER: ALICE BEADLE

Fig. 5.1   Responding to primary and secondary research enables the designer to develop their concept and generate ideas for colour, pattern and yarn. DESIGNER: LAUREN PINCHES

Creative responses

There is a natural overlap between undertaking research and generating your own ideas. In fact, the documentation of research is a creative process in itself, where the information that you encounter starts to be translated into your own work. Each mark on the page, each photograph taken, each sentence written celebrates new thought, generating a creative output of ideas. All of the artwork created at this early stage plays a major part in the development of design ideas. Corresponding annotation helps to communicate your thinking and document the decision-making process throughout the project; you can then refer back and reconnect with ideas that have since evolved during the design journey.

It is valuable to use a sketchbook to document this process. Like a projector, it can be used to transfer ideas from the mind to the page. The sketchbook is not used for research and idea generation only; the entire design journey can be documented, by including mark-making, thumbnail sketches, indications of yarn choices, and fabric-design and garment-design development. Bear in mind that the size and quality of paper will affect the way in which the sketchbook is used. Loose-leaf pages allow for a variety in terms of the scale and type of the paper being used and enables the inclusion, removal or reordering of material. Whatever the format, a sketchbook should be a positive and personal item.

Fig. 5.2   The sketchbook is a personal document within which the designer can document their thoughts visually. Mark-marking can inform fabric design, while experimentation with colour can inform the development of a palette. DESIGNER: ELLIE GUSHLOW

Media and manipulation

When documenting your research and starting to generate ideas, give consideration to the techniques and media to be used. Will you use photography, painting, drawing, collage or mark-making, or a combination of methods? Your choices will initiate the exploration of texture, pattern and colour development and have a significant impact on the development of your fabrics and garments. For example, the quality and thickness of a drawn line can inspire yarn choice, stripe potential and even garment shape. Acrylic paint can be indulgently and lavishly layered to explore colour saturation, dyeing techniques and

Fig. 5.3 An alternative approach to sketching silhouette ideas in two dimensions is to work directly on a half-scale mannequin. Paper and other materials can be collaged to create dramatic silhouette ideas. DESIGNER: LYTHIA NEENAN

Fig. 5.4 Working in three dimensions allows the designer to play around with shape, proportion and repetition. DESIGNER: LYTHIA NEENAN

the weight of a potential fabric. Bear in mind that your initial documentation can be manipulated by using image-editing CAD apps such as Adobe Photoshop. Images can be easily cropped to isolate areas of interest; filters can be added, and brightness, contrast and colour can be quickly altered. Using these tools, you can creatively enhance, distort and modify a primary image, to reflect your concept and produce contemporary artwork to influence your colour palette, fabric design and silhouette.

Responding in three dimensions

In addition to two-dimensional creative explorations in your sketchbook, you may wish to experiment with three-dimensional responses to your research. By moving into three dimensions, there is an immediate creative statement relating to shape and volume that can be translated into a potential garment idea. For example, you might manipulate paper and collaged items on a mannequin in order to investigate initial

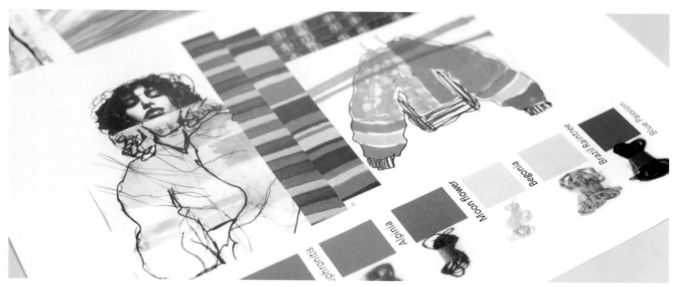

Fig. 5.5 Colour balance and proportion can be visually communicated within the portfolio by illustrating colour placement on a potential garment. Once a colour palette has been established, the designer can develop different colourways for knitted fabric designs. DESIGNER: RAVEENA FLORA

ideas relating to silhouette and form. The addition of colour, pattern and texture on to the paper enables you to explore ideas relating to fabric design before you start to knit. Another exercise could involve the manipulation of a double-sided piece of artwork, to provide inspiration for reversible design ideas or multifunctional garment concepts.

Alternatively, you might take inspiration directly from three-dimensional objects or other forms. Through the translation of these shapes on to the mannequin by using paper, plastic or found materials, garment design is encouraged to evolve through another creative route. For example, you could experiment with the dissection and remaking of a three-dimensional item such as a plastic water bottle or cardboard box. All of these three-dimensional experiments should be photographed and the resulting photographs be included in the sketchbook; these photographs can be annotated and further manipulated and may subsequently inform further three-dimensional explorations.

Colour

While responding to your research, you should start to develop a colour palette for your project. A palette typically comprises five to eight colours, to be used in various combinations and proportions. It can be influenced by a variety of sources, including trend information, client requirements or your personal inspiration. A colour palette is generally made up of darks, mids, lights and a highlight; the proportion of each group will depend on the overall look that is required. The selection of colours can be harmonious, contrasting, tonal, monochromatic, bright or neutral. A dark palette may be enhanced by including a light shade and a bright highlight. Equally, a neon palette may require a small amount of a dark shade to make the other colours stand out.

The use of a viewfinder is an excellent way to identify a potential palette. To create a simple viewfinder, a rectangle can be cut from the middle of a piece of white paper, and the resulting window that is created is then placed over an artwork or photograph. The paper masks the majority of the image, helping you to focus on the colours visible within the window, along with elements such as texture, scale and pattern. This isolated image can initiate the designing of a fabric swatch. If your viewfinder window is cut in the shape of a garment, it can be used to explore the placement of colour and detail on a potential garment design. An alternative approach is to use an image-editing app to identify colours by pixellating a key inspiration image. Once you have identified the sources of your colour inspiration, the subtle differences in tone and shade can be matched by mixing paint, by assembling colour chips from a paint chart or shade card, or by using a digital colour-picker tool. Whatever the method, you should explore the effects of different proportions of each colour within the palette, by varying the relative size of each shade.

Fig. 5.6 Inspiration in the sketchbook can be used to inform the designer's yarn choices.
DESIGNER: MERINA PELANDER

Design development: fabrics

When you have gathered a personalized collection of imagery and corresponding annotation that relates to your concept, you are ready to move into the main design phase. First, you need to choose the yarns that you will work with and develop them into original fabric designs.

Your brief will provide guidance for the process of fabric development. In the case of a commercial brief, there may be specific guidance regarding yarn types, fabric types and finishes; requirements in terms of cost and machinery will also have an impact on these decisions. A personal brief is likely to be more open, and your chosen concept may lead you to develop experimental fabrics that push technical boundaries. Whatever the situation, it is important to keep referring back to the brief and your research throughout the development process.

Choosing yarns

The visual material in a sketchbook can supply a designer with an abundance of inspiration regarding yarn choice. For example, artwork that explores the qualities of watercolours and inks could suggest translucency, light, movement or volume; these characteristics can then be related to the properties of a particular fibre or yarn type. A yarn that contains mohair or one that is loosely spun may have the tactile qualities that are required, and such a yarn could be used to produce a fabric that relates directly back to the research. An Autumn/ Winter project that takes inspiration from sculpture may suit the innovative use of felted fabrics to hold the shape and form of the garment. In this case, a lambswool yarn, which can be washed and felted, would be an appropriate choice. A project inspired by timeworn architectural structures may have involved exploratory mark-making on a variety of textural papers at the research stage; a bouclé yarn could be mixed with an elasto-meric yarn to produce a fabric with a similar appearance to that of the inspiration. As discussed in Chapter 3, other factors to be considered when selecting yarns include sustainability, price, performance and suitability for use with the intended machine and gauge.

In an ideal situation, you will be able to source appropriate types of yarn in the colours that have been specified by your colour palette. In order to identify suitable options, you need to be aware of spinners' current ranges and be prepared to undertake further focused research. Be aware that, if your designs will be produced in small quantities, your choices may be limited, as many yarns carry a minimum order. Even if this is not the case, you may find that the exact shade that you would like to use is not available. Part of the design challenge is working

within these limitations. There may be options to dye your
own colours; it might also be useful to consider plying up
finer yarns for use on coarser-gauge machines. It may even be
necessary for you to revisit your initial research and to revise
your palette. Some designers adopt an alternative approach,
utilizing surplus yarns left over from larger production runs in
previous seasons, in order to minimize textile waste. In this
case, the designer must start with the available yarn and use it
to develop a coherent story.

Selecting structures

Once you have specified a yarn to use, the next step is to
convert this yarn into a fabric that meets the requirements of
your brief and makes the most of your research. Consider which
techniques would suit your yarn: is a particular stitch needed
to allow its unique characteristics to shine? Some yarns do not
suit a complex structure; an uncomplicated knit-stitch-based
pattern could give you the desired effect. Refer back to your
concept board and think about the tactile qualities that you are
looking for and then the structure and gauge that could create
them. If your fabric needs to be soft, airy and comforting, you

might think about knitting an open tuck-structure pattern at
a relatively loose tension on a coarse-gauge machine. If you
are looking for a structure that gives stability, is dense in its
construction and allows you to experiment with form, you
might choose a stable and uncomplicated structure such as
half milano, to be knitted on a fine-gauge machine with a
smooth, classic yarn.

Cables, lace and tuck stitches relate well to research that
suggests texture and three-dimensional pattern, while multi-
coloured-patterning techniques, such as Fair Isle, intarsia and
jacquard, are excellent for experimenting with graphic elements and colour. Inspiration that has been developed through
experimentation with papers, collage and tactile media can
influence the generation of fabric designs through juxtaposed
techniques. Differences in scale, yarn and structure can be
particularly effective; for example, chunky hand-knitted or
crocheted fabrics can be combined with finer machine-knitted
fabrics with contrasting tactile characteristics. Bear in mind that
your choices may be restricted by the technology available to
you; as discussed in Chapter 4, different machine platforms
have different capabilities, with flatbed machines being the
most versatile.

Fig. 5.8 Fabric manipulation and embellishment involving latex can be used to create experimental fabrics with unusual physical qualities.
DESIGNER: CAT BRIERLEY

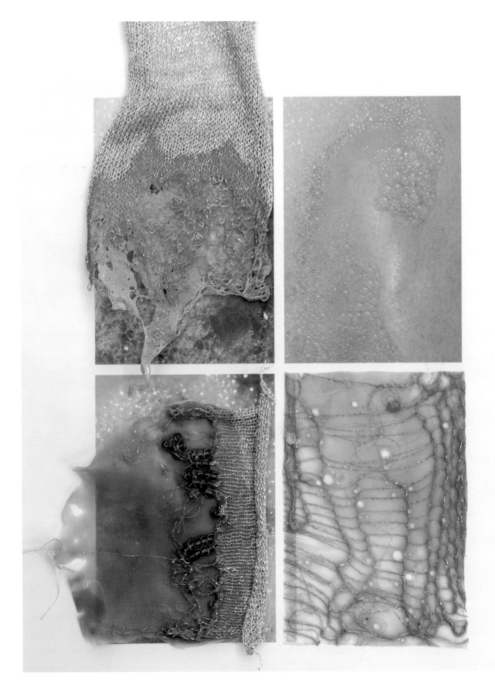

Manipulating fabrics

When designing your fabrics, you may wish to exploit the inherent three-dimensional shaping capacities of the knitted structure. Techniques, such as partial knitting and the combination of diverse structures or yarns, can be used during the knitting process to create three-dimensional forms. Inspiration may come from your initial three-dimensional experimentation; the knitted samples that you originate could, in turn, be draped on the mannequin, to develop unconventional garment designs. This approach is discussed further in Chapter 6.

Fabric manipulation need not be restricted to the knitting process; knitted fabric can also become the ground for embellishment or decoration. Both embroidery and print can be used to add texture, pattern and colour. Traditional or contemporary, abstract or representational, produced by hand or by machine,

FAIRISLE DEVELOPMENT

DIGITAL
GLITCHSCAPES

Fig. 5.9 Pattern placement and colour combinations can be explored with the use of CAD.
DESIGNER: KATE WARRINGTON

these processes add another dimension to design. Silicone and resin can be used to change the tactile qualities of a knitted fabric and may be used as a trim detail or be incorporated into or over seams. Your brief may indicate whether these various forms of fabric manipulation are relevant. Cost, machine capability and customer profile should all be considered when making decisions regarding such manipulation.

Developing your samples

When you have made initial choices regarding structures, gauges and possible manipulation, the process of fabric development can commence. A playful and experimental approach is needed in order to generate a range of potential directions. If, for example, you have identified an interest in creating a tuck structure on a 5 gauge machine, you should try out a number of possible stitch options, including use of a range of potential yarns. In order to start exploring colour, you can knit some initial samples that put the shades from your colour palette together in different stripe combinations. Play around with the stripe sizes and layouts, and mix up the colours in different ways. If you intend to design a patterned fabric, such as one featuring a Fair Isle pattern, knitting different colour combinations within a simple check pattern will similarly help you to understand how your colours will sit together.

Analysis of these initial samples will allow you to identify which options have the greatest potential for further development. During the fabric-design process, it is beneficial to keep your sketchbook with you, both to provide inspiration and to document your experiments. As you generate your samples, unexpected and exciting discoveries are likely to be made. Documenting these findings in your sketchbook, reflecting on their qualities and responding to them through further sampling will produce additional innovative fabrics.

If you knit the samples for yourself on domestic or hand-flat machines, you have an immediate result and the opportunity to adapt and make changes to the sample straight away. If you are using industrial machines, you are likely to be working in collaboration with a technician who will programme the machines to produce the samples that are required, as discussed in Chapter 4. While this additional pair of hands may make the process less immediate, once the design has been programmed, it is easy to make changes to the programme in order to try out design variations. Alternatively, through the use of CAD, it is possible to visually prototype a wide range of fabric designs without having to knit every sample. A scanned image can be modified and transformed to create a change of scale or colour, and it is possible to collage images of multiple fabrics together. At a more sophisticated level, Shima Seiki's SDS-ONE APEX3 system can be used to design diverse fabric structures and to simulate their appearance as if they were knitted with a specific yarn.

As you refine your samples, continue to think critically about how they connect to your concept and market research. It is of paramount importance that you think about how your fabrics will be worn on the body. In particular, when working with graphic patterns and fabric detailing, you should consider proportion and placement. You should also evaluate your samples to check whether the combinations and proportions of different shades from your palette are working. Be aware that you may need to design a number of colourways for each fabric. Each colourway will feature different combinations in terms of base colour, highlights and so on. If your fabric development is not progressing as you would like, it may be beneficial to revisit your research and consider changing your approach in terms of yarn, structure, colour or gauge.

While the number of fabric designs required will depend on the brief, each one must work well both individually and as a part of a coherent collection. When selecting samples for the final range, there are a number of factors to consider. For example, you should assess the balance of colour within the collection: is it as you intended? Similarly, you need to consider the range of fabric weights and the balance of patterned and plain fabrics, in order to offer choice to the customer. While you

may have spent a great deal of time on a complex, patterned design, you must not overlook the core fabrics that will play an important role in the collection. Ensure that you are not repeating similar designs, as this will create unhelpful competition within the range. It takes confidence to edit the options; you may have to make some difficult decisions. A shop report will provide insights into the way that a similar range has been structured in the past.

Design development: garments

Alongside the generation of fabric designs, the knitwear designer must develop complementary garment designs that meet the brief and respond to the research that has been gathered. In many cases, the challenge of fabric design will be tackled before the garment form is considered in any detail; at other times, the overall garment design will take the lead, with fabric design following afterwards. Whatever the situation, the two activities are likely to be intertwined to some degree, with garment design development feeding back into further fabric sampling, and vice versa.

Once again, the brief will specify parameters for the garment designs. A commercial brief might be tightly framed in terms of factors such as shape, fit, trend, cost and manufacturing techniques, while a personal brief is likely to be much more flexible. The process of developing original garment designs to meet this brief should be documented, whether in your sketchbook or an alternative format.

Generating garment ideas

Just as with the generation of ideas for knitted fabrics, your research and initial responses will provide vital inspiration for your garment designs. When developing these designs, you will need to think about various elements such as silhouette, construction, trims and placement of texture and pattern.

For some commercial briefs, elements of the garment design will already be in place. For example, you may be asked to design 'move-ons' for a particular brand; this involves taking key basic or best-selling items and updating them for the following season. If you are working directly with the brand, past-sales data may be available to identify these items. At this point, your understanding of trends will be important. The design can be updated via the inclusion of a new neckline, sleeve length, body length, body shape, trim or detail such as pockets or zips.

Fig. 5.10 Shapes, forms and textures gathered as primary research can provide a starting point for the process of garment design development.
DESIGNER: KATIE MALYON

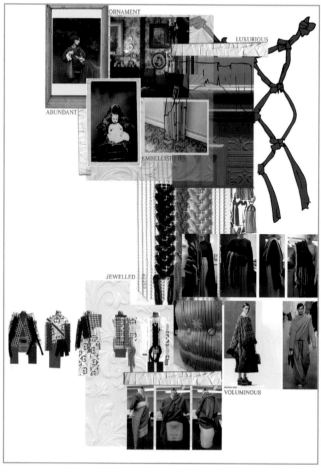

Fig. 5.11 On this portfolio page, designer Lydia Collins has documented the variety of visual research that has influenced her garment designs.

Sometimes, inspiration will come from existing garments; studying the work of other designers, for example, can instigate new design ideas. Alternatively, you may be influenced by garment styles that were identified by your trend research. There have always been varied opinions on the use of other designers' work as inspiration. Some may feel that creativity is stifled when using ideas that have been generated by someone else. Yet, it can be argued that an existing design provides a springboard to generate a new, directional and inspiring collection of ideas, made unique by the addition of a new designer's exclusive handwriting. New designs can also be informed by vintage clothing. Studying how garments have been designed and made in the past feeds a designer's understanding of their craft; therefore, methods of construction and fabric manipulation, fit and garment detail are likely to be of interest. Closures and fastenings, and pattern types and placements, can all be incorporated to new, innovative designs.

Garment inspiration can be taken from other types of research. Three-dimensional forms, for example, have clear connections to garment silhouette. A curving and sensuous piece of sculpture could influence the development of voluminous knitwear shapes with fluid, circular lines. Exploration of architectural structures, such as tower blocks, could prompt ideas for garment silhouette, trims and details including repetition and angular forms. In all cases, you should be thinking about how to translate your inspiration into the language of knitwear and considering the way in which your fabric will behave. Often this understanding will be developed through experimenting on the mannequin, as discussed in the next section.

Sketching in two and three dimensions

Thumbnail sketches are quick, loose drawings that allow the designer to capture an idea on paper. These spontaneous, energetic garment sketches may explore form and shape or placement of pattern and texture or may investigate trims and construction ideas. The designer is able to freely generate an abundance of ideas, which can be captured at any time of the day: while visiting a museum, on the commute home or by the knitting machine while experimenting with fabric samples. These initial ideas will help you to see what is working best; the most interesting aspects can then be reworked and developed. This visual expression of ideas also encourages discussion and feedback.

To take your ideas forward, try drawing the garment from different angles, on and off of the body. Take time to apply colour, indicate the fabric to be used and explore different placements for any pattern or stitch interest. Start thinking ahead to the collection as a whole, by putting your draft designs into different combinations in terms of style and colour. Ensure that you are developing enough ideas to produce a balanced and coherent collection. The addition of annotation (such as of fabric type, trim specifications or gauge of machine) will record ideas that can later be refined.

Your choice of artistic methods will affect the way in which your designs take shape. While many different media are available, a few options include:

- Pencils, charcoals, pastels: immediate and versatile; can create both a soft and delicate line and an assertive and firm line; realistic shading possibilities; can be erased and altered.
- Pens: immediate and permanent; graphic quality of line and pattern; colour choices available; intricate and precise for indication of stitch detail.
- Inks, watercolours, water-soluble pencils: fluid, transparent and soft effects indicate a lightweight, delicate and tactile fabric; intense and saturated effects indicate shine and depth of colour.
- Acrylics, oil pastels: versatile and intense; useful to indicate solid and heavy fabrics and bold colour.
- Glues, tapes and found objects: for use when textural effects are required; for example, sponge for soft, all-over texture or corrugated card for stripes, rib effects and ripples.

Fig. 5.12 Thumbnail sketches allow the designer to visualize ideas and explore how the whole collection or range might be developed. Annotation records the designer's thoughts for future reference.
DESIGNER: ALICE BEADLE

Depending on your preferred method of working, at this stage in the process, initial ideas relating to form and placement of pattern can be trialled by using paper or fabric placed on to a mannequin. You might choose to experiment with existing garments, playing with them in different combinations to generate innovative silhouette ideas. Knitted fabric swatches can be pinned on to a half-scale mannequin or placed directly on to the body. If you have already investigated aspects of your research through three-dimensional experimentation, this activity may be a continuation of that process. Throughout this experimentation, think carefully about how your knitted fabric will behave at full scale; this can vary dramatically depending on the structure, yarn and gauge. All of these experiments can be photographed, with the resulting photographs being

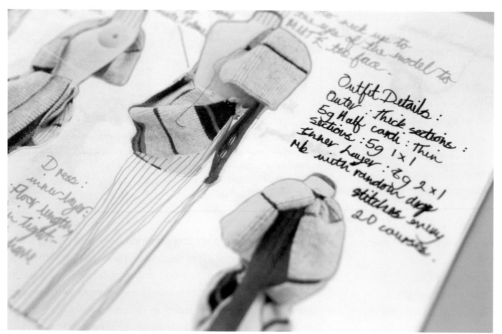

printed out and placed in a working sketchbook or layout pad. The images can then be reworked by sketching on top of the printed image or collaging elements together and redrawing the result. Thus, the design process travels from two dimensions into three dimensions, and back again.

Developing your designs

Your sketches represent initial ideas; these must be developed in order to reach a finalized design, ready to be presented or taken forward to the garment-sample stage. The sketches should be redrawn and reworked, with a focus on elements such as fit and the placement of stitch, colour and pattern. Ensure that

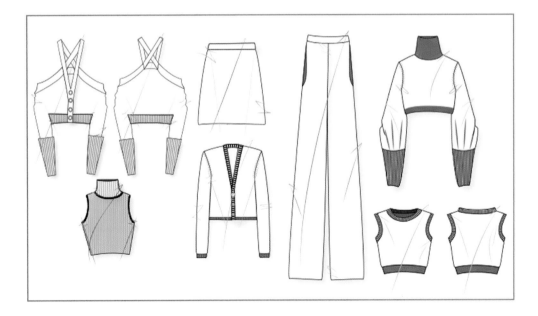

Fig. 5.15 The garment flat provides detailed information on proportions and construction, with artistic interpretation kept to a minimum.
DESIGNER: ALICE BEADLE

you are thinking about the garment in three dimensions, with consideration for how the silhouette will appear from the front, back and sides. Think carefully, too, about how the garment will be constructed, whether by using fully fashioned, seamless or cut-and-sew techniques. This will have significant implications for the final look of the garment, as well as the techniques to be used in its manufacture.

Remember to explore details such as trims and embellishment; you may need to undertake further fabric sampling in order to generate suitable options. For example, you might need to produce a working rib that will gather a loose sleeve to a tight-fitting cuff. For a commercial brief, costs will be an important consideration. Adding trims and details, such as pockets or buttons, to the garment will add to the cost – of the manufacturing process and of the garment itself – and therefore may not be possible if you are designing for a low price point.

Range sizes vary greatly. Your brief may specify a small collection of just a few garments or outfits, but it could equally require the design of dozens of styles. Whatever the case, the range needs to be carefully planned. Just as with the fabric collection, each garment must work as an individual design and also as part of the wider range. Again, it is important that designs do not compete with one another; each one must perform a different purpose within the collection. Basics should be balanced with more complex or statement pieces, and choice should be provided in terms of garment elements such as sleeve length or neckline shape, and in terms of colour. For example, you might offer the same style in a classic colour and in an accent colour from the palette, in order to provide options for the customer. Your market research will help you to reach the right balance for your target market.

Communicating your designs

When your designs are confirmed, the next stage is to communicate your collection or range as a whole. Fashion illustration allows the designer to demonstrate how the garments fit the body, how they could be worn and how the elements of the collection work together. A garment flat is a different type of drawing, with artistic interpretation kept to a minimum; it provides detailed information about the proportions and construction of the garment. These drawings are used in different ways, depending on the context. Knitwear students, for example, will combine fashion illustrations and garment flats on their portfolio pages. Designers working in the fast-paced world of mass-produced fashion are likely to communicate their ideas purely through garment flats. Both types of drawing enable the potential of a garment to be explored before it is made.

It is important to note that illustration and garment-flat drawing skills will already have been employed during the design process, in order to explore and communicate ideas. These skills are crucial for a designer. Designers working internationally may encounter language issues when attempting to communicate their garment ideas to their colleagues. In this situation, the ability to quickly sketch out a design can be a huge advantage.

Fig. 5.16 When illustrating a fashion knitwear garment, it is important for the designer to communicate the tactile qualities of the fabric as well as the overall silhouette. DESIGNER: NAN YOUNG KIM

Fashion illustration

Fashion illustration brings an attitude to a collection and should reflect both the requirements of your brief and the essence of your concept. Artistic interpretation of a collection can emphasize the handwriting and personality of the designer, for example, by the way in which the face, hands and footwear are depicted. Fashion line-ups can be creative, energetic, abstract, minimal or sophisticated. They can be executed quickly and freely or precisely and accurately, capturing every stitch and detail. Much can be communicated through the inclusion of sketchbook and contextual imagery in your illustrations; this material may help to put your designs in context. On the other hand, if working to a commercial brief, your communication may be much simpler, emphasizing the details of the designs.

It is essential for a designer to be able to draw their designs in such a way as to illustrate how the garments will be worn on the body. In order to do this, some basic rules regarding proportion need to be understood. A common approach is to draw the body length as a multiple of the head. Traditionally, a nine-head *croquis* (the French word for a sketch) is used for fashion illustration, but this can vary according to your client and the look that you are aiming to portray. When using this method, the head is drawn first and used to map out the rest of the figure. Typically, from the top of the head, two heads are measured to the chest level and armpit area, three heads to the waist, and four heads to the hips. Garments can then be portrayed in terms of how they work on the body. For example, you can visually indicate that the hem of your garment is in line with the hips and that the cuffs are in line with the elbows. By understanding and researching the body type that you are designing for, you will be able to adapt this method and 'break the rules', by experimenting with proportion and developing your own style of illustration.

There are many ways in which to illustrate a garment on a body, and, as a knitwear designer, capturing the tactile qualities of a knitted fabric is important. This depends on the appropriate choice of media; a lightweight and delicate textile may require the use of inks and watercolours, while fine liners and coloured markers may capture the effect of a garment that is structured and detailed. Collage can be an innovative and creative way to suggest garment shape and fabric type. Photographic images can be used to indicate a theme or provide elements of the figure, such as head, hands and feet. Samples of your knitted fabrics and artwork from your sketchbook can also be used effectively. When scanning in swatches, make sure that the fabrics are reduced to the required scale. These collages can be physically produced by hand or generated by using CAD.

Garment flats

While a fashion illustration evocatively describes how the garment may look on a body, a garment flat is a detailed technical drawing of the item, as the garment would look if laid flat, off of a body, and drawn to scale. This type of drawing serves a complementary, but different, purpose: to communicate the shape and construction of the garment accurately and clearly. It is vital that the flat is drawn with correctly placed style lines and seam lines and that both front and back views are provided. The details of the garment – including stitches, patterns, fashioning, embellishments, finishings and trims – should also be communicated.

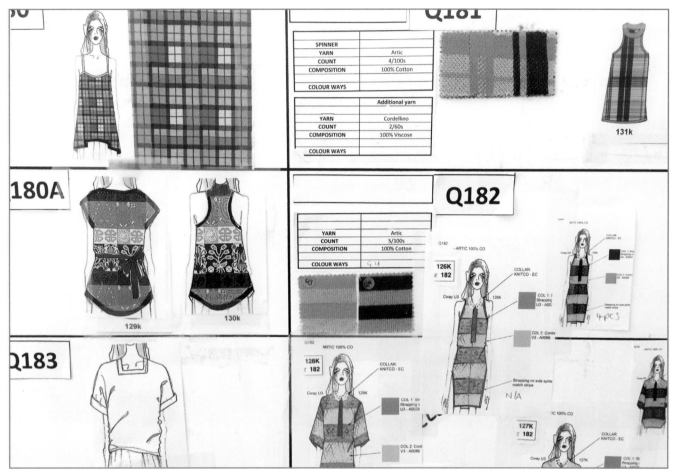

Fig. 5.17 In industry, designs are typically communicated by using garment flats, either hand drawn or produced by using CAD. The drawings are interpreted by the technical team when design samples are produced.

The garment flat serves many purposes and, in a professional setting, will be used by designers, buyers, the technical team and the sales and merchandising team. For example, flats are typically used when presenting a range of designs to a buyer. The flat also forms a key element of the tech pack and technical specification sheet, as described in Chapter 7. The flat, therefore, must contain all of the information that is needed for a technical team to be able to produce the garment as envisioned by the designer. Any mistakes in the garment flat could be translated to the sample, thereby causing problems and delays.

Garment flats can be drawn by hand; this takes practice but is a very useful skill. Fine liners enable the accurate communication of the garment shape and design details, for example, showing the difference between a fine 1×1 rib and a chunky 5×3 rib. To practise illustrating stitch structures such as cables, you can trace over photographs of actual fabrics. Once you have a drawn flat that you are happy with, this can become your template for future use, to adapt details such as length, trims and stitch placement, as required. Alternatively, flats can be produced by using a vector graphics CAD app such as Adobe Illustrator. The basic garment shape is produced by adapting an existing image or tracing a hand-drawn flat. Digital tools can then be used to add details; when working in this way, it is particularly easy to add colour and pattern, to create accurate renderings of the proposed designs.

Putting it all together

Now that you have researched, developed and drawn your knitwear collection, it needs to be presented in the appropriate format. This format will vary depending on the type of brief that you are working to. For example, you might be completing the project to develop your portfolio, for you to be ready for

Fig. 5.18 The designer's portfolio should portray the designer's individual style and handwriting. For this collection page, designer Lydia Collins has combined styled photographs of the final garments with fashion illustrations and garment flats.

Fig. 5.19 Knitwear-design students are encouraged to be experimental and creative when developing their fashion illustrations. Designer Lythia Neenan has used line effectively to communicate the textures within her collection.

interview, or be presenting a completed project to a client. If you are a student submitting your work for assessment, bear in mind that you are likely to be asked for further elements, including a research file, a sketchbook and technical documentation of the development process.

While the selection and layout of boards will depend on your own preferences and the needs of the client, you will typically need to communicate both your finished fabric designs and the final garment designs, by using textile samples, fashion illustrations and garment flats. Your illustration style, the size of the range and the type of brief will influence the way in which you put this material together. If you are designing your own range, your personal handwriting and voice should come through. Note that, in the mass-market fashion industry, range boards will typically include garment flats only; fashion illustrations are not commonly used in this context. An image-editing app can be used to reproduce the fabric image in a variety of colourways. You may also wish to include graphs, to communicate the fabric structure, and designs for any embellishment. Keep the boards coherent by placing headings in the same place and by using typography consistently. If you are working for a specific brand or client, include their logo on each board.

Optional extras include the concept and customer-profile boards that are described in Chapter 2. You may wish to include a design-generation board to communicate the method that you have used to develop your final garment ideas, which could include thumbnail sketches, initial fabric samples, images of work on the mannequin and prototype-garment (toile) development. Individual design boards can also be produced, communicating a single style with accompanying technical detail. If you are taking your design project through to finished garments, you may have the opportunity to document your designs in a photo shoot. The styling of your garments is another opportunity for creativity and should link back to your design concept. The resulting images can then be presented on further boards within the portfolio or as a stand-alone lookbook.

It is increasingly important for designers to promote themselves online, by showcasing their work on portfolio platforms such as Arts Thread, networking sites such as LinkedIn, individual websites, blogs and social media. Give consideration to how you will communicate your work in these digital spaces; each one may have different requirements and expectations in terms of image type, size and style. Think carefully about the tactile

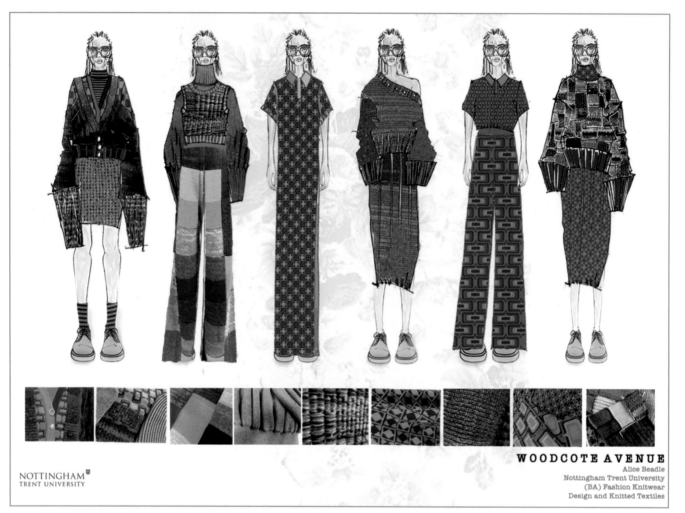

Fig. 5.20 The final line-up board should be a showpiece, visually communicating the collection and highlighting the designer's skills. DESIGNER: ALICE BEADLE

elements of your portfolio when presenting your work online. If you are scanning swatches, ensure that you scan them at a high resolution and reproduce the fabrics at the correct scale.

This final stage regarding the visual communication of all of your hard work should be a celebration and an enjoyable experience. If you have constantly documented the design process then the job of putting it all together at the end will be much easier! If you have developed a method of presentation that works well, there is no reason why this format cannot be used for further projects, adapting content as necessary to suit each new brief.

Fig. 5.21 Lookbook photography provides the opportunity to showcase the design and craftsmanship of a finished outfit. The styling should link back to the design concept. DESIGNER: CHARLOTTE BULL. PHOTOGRAPHER: LORETTA KERRY, LRK PHOTOGRAPHY

CHAPTER 6

PATTERN CUTTING AND SILHOUETTE

by Juliana Sissons

Introduction

Garment-making can be seen as being somewhat similar to the practice of sculpture. The first considerations of design often relate to the silhouette: how is the piece going to sit on the body? Will it emphasize the body's natural curves or will it hide or even distort the body shape? Unlike clothes made from woven fabrics, knitwear offers a unique potential for a garment to fit close to the skin, while remaining flexible and comfortable to wear. Depending on the stitch, gauge and yarn that are used, designers of knitwear can also create voluminous and striking shapes that sit away from the body.

This chapter introduces several different ways to approach the process of creating a pattern for a knitted garment. A flat pattern can be produced, using a block template as a starting point. Draping fabric on a mannequin is another classic approach, which can be used to make close-fitting or more fluid silhouettes. Once a pattern has been created, it must be converted into instructions to guide the creation of the knitted pieces. A more organic methodology fuses the pattern-cutting process with the development of the knitted fabric, with the

characteristics of the swatch dictating the shape of the garment. Yet another strategy is to use geometric shapes to create unconventional silhouettes and eliminate the waste that is associated with cut-and-sew production.

Flat-pattern cutting

The conventional way to produce a three-dimensional garment is to create a two-dimensional pattern. For a sweater, this will typically take the form of front, back and sleeve pattern pieces. The aim when creating this flat pattern is to realize the designer's vision, as communicated in the garment flat and fashion illustration. This visual information must be referred to throughout the pattern-cutting process, in order to ensure that the proportions, fit and any stitch or pattern placement correspond with the intended design.

This section describes the process of using a block, or template, as a starting point and making adaptations to it to produce the finished pattern. In industrial settings, a different strategy is commonly used: a size chart is produced that specifies the dimensions of the finished garment, and this is used to produce the pattern. Although the method described here relates to blocks and patterns that are created by using paper, digital CAD pattern-cutting tools can also be used.

Juliana Sissons' sculptural dress, inspired by armour, was created by using wire, cotton and lurex yarns. PHOTOGRAPHER: REBECCA ZEPHYR THOMAS

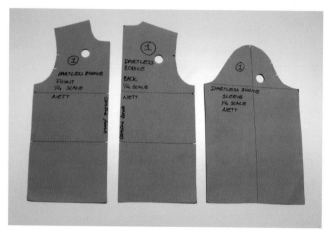

Fig. 6.1 Blocks, which look like simple pattern pieces, can be used as a starting point for creating a flat pattern.

Blocks

Blocks look like simple pattern pieces and are made for basic garment types, such as a sweater, cardigan or trousers. Pieces for each garment component, such as front, back and sleeve, are provided. Blocks can be created for tight-fitting or easy-fitting silhouettes; unlike blocks for woven fabrics, darts are not used, as this form of shaping is not appropriate for knitwear, which stretches to fit the body. Many blocks for knitted fabric include ease: room within the garment that allows the body to move. This means that the width of the block will typically be a few centimetres wider than the relevant body measurement. However, because of the inherent stretch within the knitted structure, it is possible for a block to be smaller than the size of the body for which it was designed; this is referred to as negative ease. The amount of ease or negative ease depends on the extensibility of the knitted fabric and how tightly the garment is intended to fit. The block for a close-fitting dress to be made from a fine-gauge, high-stretch fabric would be smaller than the relevant body measurements, while a block for an easy-fitting sweater that is intended to be made from a bulky knitted fabric would be significantly larger.

In the knitwear industry, blocks are made in a sample size, drafted from a standard size chart that gives measurements for different parts of the body. Designers and retailers often have their own blocks that have been adapted to suit their customer, preferred fit and signature styles. Alternatively, bespoke blocks can be drafted by using a set of personal measurements. A block can also be made by taking the measurements of an existing garment or through the deconstruction of an old garment. If deconstructing, the item should be taken apart and the individual pieces carefully steamed flat, without stretching the fabric. The pieces can then be traced around and the shapes corrected where needed, for example, to ensure that seam lengths will match for the pieces that will be adjacent and seamed together within the assembled garment.

Developing the pattern

The first step in developing the pattern is to choose the most appropriate block, considering the garment type, fabric characteristics and desired fit. The templates (such as front, back and sleeve) are traced on to paper, and the pattern is then developed by making adaptations to these basic shapes. To achieve the intended silhouette, alterations may involve extending or shortening the length of panels and adding or taking away fullness. Standard pattern-cutting techniques can be used. For example, the technique of cut-and-spread can be used to create a flared shape: to do this, you would cut through an existing pattern piece from one edge to the other, and open it out to form a wider shape.

During this process, it is crucial to keep in mind the characteristics of the knitted fabric to be used: how it will stretch, sculpt or drape. You should also think about the way that the garment will be constructed, for example, how raw edges will be finished if you are using cut-and-sew methods. Bear in mind that the garment panels will need to be knitted to shape for fully fashioned construction and that some shapes are easier to knit than others. Consider the direction of the knitting; for flared shapes, it may be most appropriate to use the partial-knitting technique and place the knitted panel sideways on the body. The width of a knitted fabric is limited by the size of the machine, so you will also need to make sure that the panels do not exceed this maximum width. You may need to think creatively, to work within this limitation. Indicate on the pattern any areas of pattern or stitch detail, with consideration for the proportions that are communicated on the two-dimensional design. Pay particular attention to the cast-on edges of the garment: will these be ribs, which typically pull the silhouette in, or another edging, such as a roll-edge trim?

Drafting basic bodice and sleeve blocks

These instructions guide you through the process of drafting blocks for a basic bodice with a classic set-in sleeve, suitable for knitwear. This involves building a full-size, customized version of the diagrams provided, by drawing the lines and points in the order specified and by using measurements to suit your requirements in terms of size. Ease is incorporated during the drafting process and can be varied as required. As a example, measurements are provided for a woman who would wear a standard UK size 12 garment. Seam allowances are not included in the block.

Standard size 12 body measurements: bust 88cm (34½in); nape-to-waist length (back length) 40cm (15¾in); armhole depth 21cm (8¼in); neck size 37cm (14½in); shoulder 12.5cm (5in); back width 34.5cm (13½in); arm length 58.5cm (23in); top arm 28.5cm (11in); wrist circumference 18cm (7in).

Basic bodice

- 1–2 = nape-to-waist-length measurement plus 2cm (¾in) ease; draw a perpendicular line (which is widely described as 'square across') from point 1 and from point 2
- 1–3 = one-fifth of neck measurement
- 1–4 = armhole-depth measurement plus 3cm (1¼in)
- 4–5 = square across from point 4 to one-fourth of bust measurement plus 0.75cm (¼in) ease
- 5–6 = square down from point 5 to establish point 6 where the line squared across from point 2 is met
- 4–7 = half of back-width measurement plus 0.75cm (¼in) ease
- 7–8 = square up from point 7 to establish point 8 where the line squared across from point 1 is met
- 8–9 = 3cm (1¼in) (shoulder-slope depth); join point 3 to point 9
- 7–10 = 3cm (1¼in)
- 5–10 = draw a curve

You now have half of a back-body draft. Trace a copy for the half-front block, and draw in a front neckline from point 3, as required. Check that the front and back neck measurements do not measure less than half of the full neck measurement.

Classic set-in sleeve

- 1–2 = arm-length measurement plus 2cm (¾in) ease; square across from point 1 and from point 2
- 1–3 = half of top-arm measurement plus 1.5cm (½in) ease; square down from point 3 to establish point 4 where the line squared across from point 2 is met

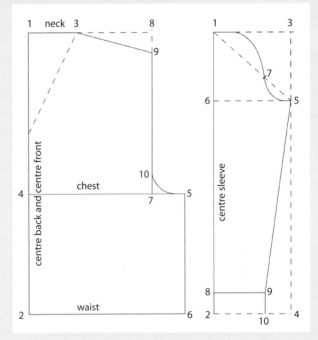

Fig. 6.2 Blocks for a basic bodice with classic set-in sleeves.

- 1–5 = draw a line equal to the armhole-depth measurement from point 1 to touch the line running from point 3 to point 4
- 5–6 = square across from point 5 to point 6
- 5–7 = one-third of the length of the line running from point 5 to point 1
- 5–1 = draw a curve touching the line running from point 5 to point 6 for approximately 3cm (1¼in), then curve up to touch point 7 and curve higher to finish this line at point 1; measure this sleeve-head curve, and adjust this line as necessary to achieve the same size of armhole as on the bodice
- 2–8 = square up from point 2 for cuff depth of 6cm (2½in); square across from point 8 for half of wrist-circumference measurement to establish point 9
- 9–10 = square down from point 9 for cuff depth of 6cm (2½in)
- 9–5 = join with a straight line

You now have a half-sleeve block; the other half of the sleeve is mirrored from the centre-sleeve line of the block.

Fig. 6.3 When developing a pattern, the designer is aiming to realize the vision communicated in the garment flat and fashion illustration.

Sleeves

An important element of a knitted garment is the sleeves; there are various ways in which these can be constructed. A set-in sleeve is joined to the body by a seam that runs from the armpit to the edge of the shoulder. The set-in-sleeve block will have been drafted to match the size and depth of the armhole on the matching bodice block; if the armhole has been lowered during pattern development, the sleeve head must be widened to match the measurement of the armhole. Further variations to a set-in sleeve head can be made, depending on the desired outcome. For example, if a puffed sleeve head is required, it will need to be made deeper and wider by using the cut-and-spread technique. The silhouette of the lower part of the sleeve can also be adapted. Again, it is important to consider the knitted fabric that will be used to produce the garment. If the fabric is thick and heavy, a puffed sleeve head would be too bulky, and it would be difficult to fit into the armhole. Flared sleeves work well with fine, floaty knitted fabrics that can enhance drape.

Other traditional knitwear sleeve constructions include the drop-shoulder sleeve, which is similar to a set-in sleeve but without any shaping of the armhole or sleeve head and creates a boxy silhouette. The saddle-shoulder sleeve has a shaped shoulder strap 'grown on' to the sleeve head and placed over the shoulder, finishing at the neck edge. The raglan-sleeve style has a seam line running diagonally from the underarm to the neckline; again, a part of the body is grown on to the sleeve head to create the pattern shape.

For a kimono sleeve, the sleeve and body are merged entirely. The angle of the shoulder slope and depth of the armhole area will vary depending on the design. If the design requires the sleeve to slope at a steep angle, an underarm gusset may be required, in order to allow for more movement of the arm. This type of sleeve is knitted as one with the body section, so measurements will need to be taken from both the widest and the longest parts of the pattern piece, to check whether it can be knitted in full on the selected machine, either vertically or horizontally.

Necklines, collars and openings

There are several basic necklines that are commonly used in knitwear; most knitwear designs can be identified as one of these shapes, for the purposes of pattern cutting. When developing the pattern, it is important to always consider the size of the neck opening, especially on close-fitting styles, to ensure that it will fit over the head. Some necklines, such as a V-neck or crew neck, are cut into the body pattern and usually finished with a trim, such as a sandwich trim or rib trim. These shapes can be varied by altering the overall shape, back neck width and front neck drop. The depth of the trim can also be varied, to give different aesthetic effects.

Other necklines require a separate collar to be knitted and attached. For a flat-collar design, such as a sailor-style collar, the shape can be based on the main-body pattern. The necklines of the front- and back-body pieces are placed together and traced off, along with the outside line of the collar shape. A flat-collar pattern piece can be used as a starting point for producing a frilled-collar pattern piece, by adding flare by using the cut-and-spread technique; the resulting shape would need to be produced by using partial knitting. A flat or frilled collar is knitted as a second fabric layer and attached at the neckline.

A stand collar rises up from the neckline. It may have a single element, as in a traditional rib turtleneck collar; it can be constructed with additional length to fold over, as in a polo neck; or it may fold and fall away from the neck, as in the collar on a polo shirt. Patterns for these collars are based on rectangles; the length is determined by the neckline-circum-

Fig. 6.4 This sweater by designer Alice Beadle features a polo neck, gathered drop-shoulder sleeve and ribbed cuffs.
PHOTOGRAPHER: LOTTIE HOWARD

Fig. 6.5 This chunky-gauge knitted outfit by Alice Beadle has an asymmetric skirt and top, with an oversized, extended button stand made from separate pieces of strapping. PHOTOGRAPHER: LOTTIE HOWARD

ference measurement (and possible button-stand width), and the height corresponds to the shape required. Grown-on-collar types include the roll neck, the shawl collar, the cowl and the revere; these shapes are extended from the body panels, with the length and the proportions varying according to the design.

Openings, such as a front zip or a buttoned fastening, also need to be considered at the pattern-cutting stage. If the buttons and buttonholes are to be positioned on the main-body panels, the pattern needs to have a button-stand allowance grown on to the centre-front edge; this overlap provides room for both the buttons and the buttonholes to be placed on the centre-front line. This style would require a knitted strap to be stitched flat behind the opening, to give support to the buttons and buttonholes. However, if the buttons and buttonholes are positioned on a narrow strapping stole (placket), no allowance is required. The same is true for zip trims.

Testing the pattern

With all of these elements in place, the pattern is ready to be tested via a shell-shape toile. This is a prototype, usually made in jersey fabric of a similar weight to that to be used for the finished garment. Placed on a body or mannequin, it can be used to analyse the silhouette, fit and proportions of the garment in relation to the two-dimensional design. Further adjustments to the pattern are often needed; significant changes will require a second toile to be put together. Note that seam allowances will need to be added to the pattern, appropriate for the selected method of construction.

Calculating knitting instructions

After the blocks have been developed into a finished pattern, the instructions for knitting the garment panels can be calculated. In industry, this process would be undertaken by a specialist technician, typically by using a CAD/CAM system. Students and designers working on a small scale are much more likely to carry out the calculations themselves. The instructions may take the form of a diagram or written directions, or a combination of the two. If you are producing instructions for someone else to follow, standard terminology must be used, in order to transmit the instructions clearly.

Stitch and row densities

The first step in calculating the knitting instructions is to produce a tension swatch of at least 20cm (8in) square, by working with the correct yarn, machine gauge and tension. This swatch is used to determine the density of the stitches and rows (wales and courses, respectively) in the fabric. These are usually counted over 10cm (4in) horizontally (stitches) and vertically (rows). If a larger swatch is knitted, densities can be recorded from multiple positions; an average of these densities will give a more accurate result. The stitch count and row count should then be divided to give figures for stitches per centimetre and rows per centimetre. These figures are used to calculate the instructions for a panel of a given size. For example, if a stitch density is counted as thirty stitches and forty rows to 10cm when divided by ten, this gives three stitches and four rows per 1cm. For coarser-gauge fabrics, this is unlikely to be a whole number, but it should not be rounded. While centimetres are used in these instructions, note that imperial units can be used throughout the calculation process, if preferred.

Garment-blank calculations

If the garment will be constructed by using the cut-and-sew technique, all that needs to be calculated are the sizes of the rectangular garment blanks from which the pattern shapes will be cut. In an industrial setting, these will be knitted to the exact dimensions that are required for each panel, in order to minimize waste. If you are creating a sample garment in a studio environment, you may wish to make your panel a little bigger in each direction, to allow for any shrinkage.

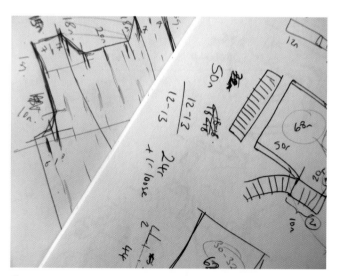

Fig. 6.6 Instructions can be calculated either on a full-scale pattern or on a smaller diagram. Rough working out must be converted into clearly communicated instructions that use standard terminology.

For example, you may wish to knit a body panel that is 50cm wide. Using the stitch-density figures from the presented example, this width of fabric would be produced by casting on and knitting 150 stitches (50cm × 3 stitches per 1cm). If you wanted a panel length of 65cm in total, which includes a rib welt of 5cm in depth, based on the example row density, you would knit 240 rows (60cm × 4 rows per 1cm) of the body fabric. To calculate the number of rows required for the 5cm rib welt to be knitted at the start of the panel, you would need to knit a sample of the relevant structure and measure the row density.

Shaped-panel calculations

If you are knitting panels to shape for fully fashioned construction, the calculation of the knitting instructions will be more complex. Your pattern outline will often include curves or diagonal lines, such as for necklines, shoulders, armholes and sleeves. Any fashioning (narrowing) or widening of the panels will require decreases and increases to be calculated. To start, write on to the pattern (or a scale representation) all of the width and length measurements. Next, divide the pattern piece by using horizontal lines; you are aiming to break the shape into rectangular sections, which can be knitted without shaping, and sections with diagonal shaping. Curves must be converted to diagonals. If the pattern piece has a large curve, such as in the case of a set-in sleeve head or a scoop neckline, it is advisable to divide it into two or three sections with different diagonal angles, in order to more closely match the shape. The dimensions of these sections can then be written in, and all of the measurements can be converted into stitches and rows by using the relevant density figures.

For rectangular sections of the garment, the conversion into stitches and rows is straightforward; it can be worked out in the same way as for a garment blank, as described previously. For areas with shaping, the calculations require more consideration. Focusing on each shaped section in turn, measure the width and height of the diagonal; by converting these into stitches and rows, you can see how many stitches need to be decreased or increased and the number of rows that these shapings need to be distributed over. The number of rows available should then be divided by the number of stitches that need to be decreased or increased, in order to reveal the number of rows that need to be knitted between each shaping. If the figures are not easily divisible, the numbers can be rounded up or down for ease of calculation, and any stitches or rows that are left over can be added at a suitable position. Bear in mind that double or triple decreases can be used, by moving a group of stitches in by two or three positions, rather than by one stitch as for a single decrease; in this case, the number of rows between each decrease would be doubled or tripled, respectively, to achieve a consistent angle of shaping.

If you are combining different knitted structures within the same panel, be aware that they may have different stitch and row densities. For example, tuck structures tend to produce a wider knitted fabric than do single-jersey structures worked over the same number of needles, while ribs typically contract more than does single jersey. Depending on how you want the fabric to behave, you may need to introduce shapings to counteract this effect. If you are using the partial-knitting technique, you will need to think carefully about the dimensions of the piece. Calculating the number of rows needed for the shortest section of the panel and the number of rows needed for the longest section of the panel will help you to work out the rate at which needles should be placed on hold.

Draping on a mannequin

An alternative way to create the pattern for a knitted garment is to drape on a mannequin, also known as a stand. This may involve the classic technique of modelling, or working in a more open-ended way with samples of knitted fabric, to investigate their potential for creating sculptural shapes. When draping in this manner, the shape-making process is exploratory, forming an integral element of the development of the design.

Using classic modelling techniques

Modelling involves draping a piece of fabric on a mannequin, to produce a silhouette that is then converted into a flat pattern. More immediate outcomes are achieved by working in this way than for flat-pattern cutting; the fabric is manipulated, moulded and shaped by hand until the design is finalized. The best-known designers to use the draping technique were Madeleine Vionnet, from the 1920s, and Madame Alix Grès, from the 1930s; still to this day, designers look back to these designers' achievements for technical inspiration in design. This is as relevant for knitwear as for garments made from woven fabric.

The characteristics of the fabric to be used for the final garment will significantly affect the silhouette that can be created. Thick, densely constructed or hairy knitted fabrics tend to produce more structured outcomes, while a draped silhouette can be achieved through the use of a fine-gauge knitted fabric with a loose construction. Therefore, it is important to drape with a fabric that has similar characteristics to those of the knitted fabric to be used for the final garment, in order to accurately mimic the behaviour of this final garment fabric. The knitted fabrics most commonly used for the stages of draping and toiling (the making and adjusting of toiles) are the different weights of single- and double-jersey fabrics. Alternatively, a large piece of the final garment fabric can be knitted and draped, allowing the nature of that particular knitted fabric to dictate the garment design.

To start the draping process, the fabric is secured to the mannequin by using pins. To ensure that the pattern is balanced and does not swing one way or the other, the fabric must be positioned properly at the outset. To do so, place the vertical wale of the fabric (equivalent to the grain of a woven fabric) on the centre-front line of the mannequin, and pin the fabric securely in place. Make sure that the fabric is placed at least 10cm (4in) above the neckline at the top of the body;

Sample shaping calculations

These simple patterns are intended to illustrate the general principles of calculating knitting instructions for a shaped pattern piece. They feature a stitch density of 3 stitches and 4 rows per centimetre. (Note: because the stitch density and row density are calculated per centimetre, measurements are given in centimetres; if preferred, the entire procedure can be carried out by using imperial units.)

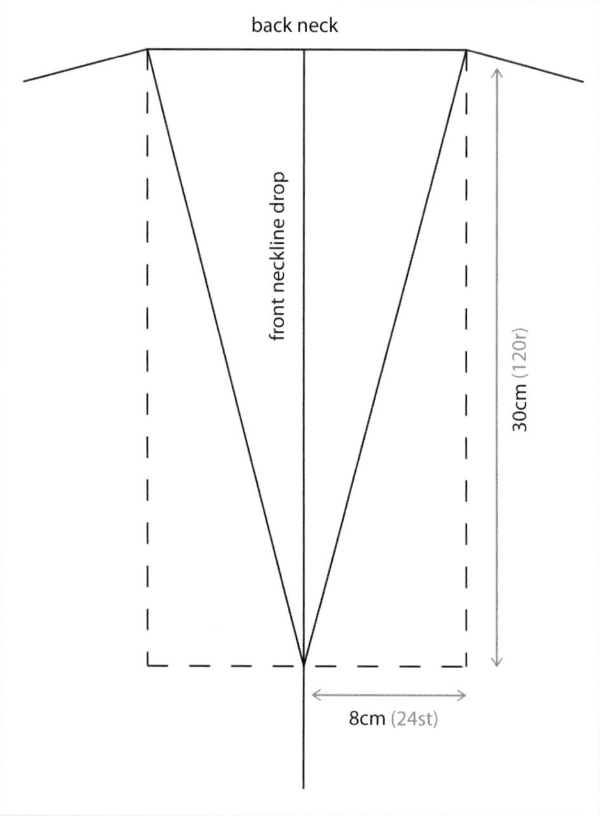

Neckline

The illustration represents a V-neck garment with a back neck width of 16cm, but, as the shaping is constructed on one side at a time, this has been divided by two, so 8cm on each side. This calculates as 24 stitches to be decreased on each side of the front neck shape (8cm × 3 stitches per 1cm).

The front neckline drop is 30cm. This calculates as 120 rows to be knitted on each side of the front neck shape (30cm × 4 rows per 1cm).

To calculate the decrease of 24 stitches over 120 rows, divide 120 (rows available) by 24 (stitches to be decreased) = 5; the neckline therefore requires a decrease of 1 stitch every 5 rows on each side of the V-neck. Alternatively, a double decrease could be worked every 10 rows or a triple decrease every 15 rows.

Fig. 6.7   Example of a V-neck, with dimensions – as measurements and numbers of stitches (st) or rows (r) – for the diagonal to be produced (by decreasing, in this instance).

Armhole

The illustration displays a typical set-in-sleeve armhole pattern. After knitting the body section, shaping for the base of the armhole begins. The curve drawn on the pattern measures 5cm wide by 3cm high. This calculates as a decrease of 15 stitches (5cm × 3 stitches per 1cm) over 12 rows (3cm × 4 rows per 1cm).

To calculate the decrease, divide 12 (rows available) by 15 (stitches to be decreased) = 1 (after rounding to the nearest whole number), with 3 stitches left over; in this case, the 3 stitches that are left over should be decreased at the start of the curve, followed by a decrease of 1 stitch every row for 12 rows. Alternatively, a double decrease could be worked every 2 rows. After this shaping, the armhole is knitted straight until the shoulder shaping begins.

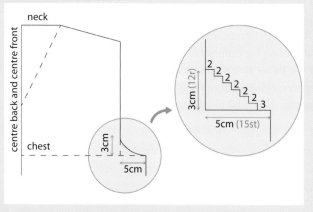

Fig. 6.8   Example of an armhole, converted from a smooth curve into graphical instructions for shaping.

Sleeve head

After knitting the main sleeve up to the underarm point, the sleeve-head shaping begins. Although the diagram displays only the measurements on one side, both sides of the sleeve head are decreased at the same time. To allow the calculation of the required shapings, a line is drawn down the centre of the sleeve pattern, and the sleeve head is divided into diagonal sections according to the curve of the crown. The number of stitches and rows to be decreased within each of these sections are calculated.

Start by binding off a number of underarm stitches to form the horizontal section of the sleeve-head shape; in this case, the horizontal section is 3cm wide, which calculates as 9 stitches (3cm × 3 stitches per 1cm).

The first shaping section measures 3cm wide by 5cm high. This calculates as a decrease of 9 stitches (3cm × 3 stitches per 1cm) over 20 rows (5cm × 4 rows per 1cm). To calculate the decrease, divide 20 (rows available) by 9 (stitches to be decreased) = 2, with 2 rows left over. Decrease 1 stitch every 2 rows for 18 rows, then knit 2 rows.

The second shaping section measures 2cm wide by 7cm high. This calculates as a decrease of 6 stitches (2cm × 3 stitches per 1cm) over 28 rows (7cm × 4 rows per 1cm). To calculate the decrease, divide 28 (rows available) by 6 (stitches to be decreased). This gives a figure of 4.67; the best solution is to use double decreases. Decrease 2 stitches every 9 rows for 27 rows, then knit 1 row.

The third shaping section measures 3cm wide by 2.5cm high. This calculates as a decrease of 9 stitches (3cm × 3 stitches per 1cm) over 10 rows (2.5cm × 4 rows per 1cm). To calculate the decrease, divide 10 (rows available) by 9 (stitches to be decreased) = 1, with 1 row left over. Decrease 1 stitch every row for 9 rows, then knit 1 row. Alternatively, decrease 2 stitches every 2 rows for 8 rows, then decrease 1 stitch in 2 rows.

Finally, bind off 12 stitches (4cm × 3 stitches per 1cm) at the top of the crown.

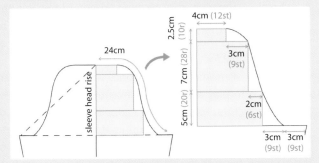

Fig. 6.9 Example of a sleeve head, with the large curve broken down into sections. The shaping for each section is calculated separately.

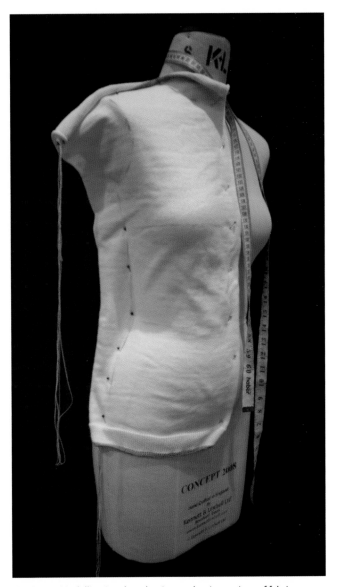

Fig. 6.10 Modelling involves draping or shaping a piece of fabric on a mannequin to produce a silhouette that is then converted into a flat pattern. It is the only pattern-making system that relies solely on fabric for the creation of designs.

this excess of fabric can be used to create shape around the neck and shoulder. A horizontal course (equivalent to the cross-grain of a woven fabric) should then be pinned in position along the bust line, to finish at the underarm point. You are now ready to model the fabric over the body of the mannequin.

A tight-fitting pattern with negative ease can be created by using classic modelling techniques; the fabric is stretched in order to hug the body. When working in this way, it is easier to model your fabric on one side of the body only, as the other

Fig. 6.11 While Jacaranda Brain's catwalk knitwear pieces are highly refined, her design process often starts with the construction of large pieces of knitted fabric. By modelling these pieces on the mannequin, she is able to investigate their sculptural potential.
PHOTOGRAPHER: SIMON ARMSTRONG FOR NOTTINGHAM TRENT UNIVERSITY

If you wish to create a looser fit, rather than for the fabric to be fitting closely to the mannequin, you will drape the fabric into the shape required. Fabrics can be modelled to fit closely in some areas and not in others or be completely draped to fall away from the body in loose, oversized folds. These silhouettes are often stabilized through a fitted area being included around the neck and shoulders. You must evaluate the drape at each step of the draping process, in order to ensure that the lines of the fabric are in balance.

Before taking the draped fabric off of the mannequin, ensure that all design and fitting lines are marked on the fabric. Centre front and centre back; side seams; bust, waist and hip lines; and shoulder lines and neck position are all important points of reference when translating the draped fabric shape into a paper pattern. The draped pieces are then unpinned and traced off on to paper. Make sure that the centre front and centre back are aligned to vertical lines on the pattern paper and then carefully refine the pattern. Make sure that the shoulder lengths measure the same on the front and the back and that the side seams are of the same length, with matching bust, waist and hip points. To sustain the correct balance between the front and back sections of pattern, check that the centre-front and centre-back lines are accurate and that the bust and waist lines are positioned at right angles to these lines. The instructions for knitting the pattern can then be calculated, as explained in the previous section.

Using three-dimensional fabrics

Another approach to draping on a mannequin is to work with your own knitted fabric samples, allowing the silhouette created to inform the design of the garment. This method merges pattern cutting with textile-shaping skills, allowing the designer to move back and forth between the machine and the mannequin. A half-scale mannequin may be used, in order to enable the use of relatively small swatches. The most exciting fabrics to work with will be those with three-dimensional qualities that provide potential for creating striking silhouettes.

One way of making knitted fabrics with sculptural characteristics is to play around with inventive combinations of yarn and structure. For example, a couple of simple stripes of elastomeric yarn in a plain, cotton knitted fabric can create a fantastic silhouette when the resulting fabric is taken off of the machine, because the elastomeric yarn suddenly contracts and allows the cotton to form a billowing shape. Even simple changes in structure – from rib to tuck, for example – create a

side can be mirrored later. Moving the fabric in an outwards direction, away from the centre front, smooth the fullness around the neckline, shoulder and armhole; mark in the neck, shoulder and armhole lines with chalk, pin the fabric into place, and cut off the surplus fabric. Adjust and pin under the arm, if necessary, and form a side seam by pinning along the side of the body of the mannequin. At the waist level, work outwards from the centre front to smooth as much fullness as possible into the side seam, in order to avoid creating a dart; mark and repin along the side seam. Cut off the surplus fabric. This procedure is repeated on one side of the back of the mannequin.

Fig. 6.12 Designer Stefan Efobi has used an inlay technique to trap waxed cords within a double-jersey knit. The resulting fabric provides a structured shape that can be moulded on the mannequin, to investigate the design concept further.

Fig. 6.13 Jacaranda Brain has developed a form of tubular pocketing stuffed with cotton wool, to create structured fabrics that are able to stand on their own. PHOTOGRAPHERS: EMILY DRINKELD / HAO FU

step change in width that can be an effective means of creating shape. Weaving and inlay techniques can be used to incorporate yarns into the fabric that would be too thick or textured for the gauge of machine in use, opening up further sculptural possibilities. Designer Derek Lawlor pushes boundaries in this way; his magnificent pieces have rubber cords woven into the knitted fabric in layered sections, to build voluminous silhouettes on otherwise tight-fitting garments.

Another method is to exploit the knitted structure's inherent capacity for three-dimensional shaping. The partial-knitting technique, for example, is particularly versatile and can be used to create a variety of forms. As discussed earlier in this chapter, it can be used to create fabrics with godet-like flares; a sample of this type could be pinned on to the mannequin in various positions to develop the basis for a garment design, whether fitted or draped. The same technique can also be used to engineer sock-heel-type shapes, straps and loops of various sizes within the fabric panel. These sculptural elements can be repeated, combined and varied in scale, to create voluminous or subtle silhouettes.

Fig. 6.15 This piece by Jacaranda Brain incorporates a combination of techniques, creating a striking garment that both follows and extends the lines of the body. PHOTOGRAPHER: SIMON ARMSTRONG FOR NOTTINGHAM TRENT UNIVERSITY

Geometric methods

As further alternatives to the conventional technique of flat-pattern cutting, conceptual approaches to pattern-making can be adopted that explore geometric shapes and the notion of zero waste. Placing the emphasis on the shape to be knitted rather than the form of the human body, these shape-making methodologies can quickly generate unique prototypes for further development.

Working with geometric shapes

A geometric approach to pattern cutting takes the cutter away from the rules and restrictions of conventional techniques. Iconic designers have chosen to work in this way; the couture garments created by Cristóbal Balenciaga, for example, were often based on circles and rectangles, made three-dimensional by intricate gathering and seaming. Issey Miyake's 'beauty when folded' concept, meanwhile, has led him to create intricately

Fig. 6.14 Jacaranda Brain's knitwear demonstrates use of the partial-knitting technique to great effect. The textured front of this dress features a repeated double-sock-heel shape, while the sleeves feature partially knitted straps and application of a cast-on/cast-off technique. PHOTOGRAPHERS: EMILY DRINKELD / HAO FU

folded geometric pieces that unfold to reveal unexpected three-dimensional forms. Because of the simplicity of the principle, it is exciting to consider working with geometric shapes for knitwear. The knitted structure is well suited to creating these shapes; the shapes can be used as simple forms, or additional cuts can be made and the fabric be twisted, pleated and multiplied to add additional detail and volume. If desired, geometric shapes can be explored on a half-scale mannequin and then graded to full size after the desired effect has been achieved.

The square is one of the simplest geometric shapes and is especially well suited to the knitted structure. Although it has uniformity, when draped on a mannequin, it can reveal a soft volume with movement. If multiple squares are used together in one garment, a larger silhouette can be created and a layered, concertina-style drape achieved. These shapes could be draped from the neckline or waistline to develop unusual starting points for sleeves, sweaters, cardigans, dresses or trousers. The rectangle is a stable shape within garment design; elongated and streamlined effects can be achieved through its longer lines than those of a square. Volume can be formed through the manipulation of pleats and folds, as well as structures, and the drape can be twisted across or around the body.

While the triangle can be seen simply as being a quarter of the solid square, if a single triangle is placed at an angle or suspended by a point, a frill-like effect can be achieved, through the drape of the free-flowing fabric. A large triangle can be used to create dramatic shapes on the body, by exploring the angles of the shape and the stretch of the knitted fabric. If the triangle partly fits close to the body and partly drapes loosely, interesting contrasts of fit and volume can be achieved within one piece. If multiple triangles are placed together in the same direction, an unconventionally shaped skirt can be achieved through fitting at the waist or hips and allowing the natural flow of volume to extend to the hemline.

The continuous outline of the circle can be used to dictate interesting seam line placements across the body of the garment; it can be easily modelled to fit the body, making use of the fabric's stretch for a close fit. Multiple circles connected together along half of the outside edge to form concertina-style shapes would drape freely, offering another type of sculptural formation. These experiments could provide interesting ideas for detailed pockets, collars and sleeves of different shapes, as well as whole-body silhouettes. The partial-knitting technique offers a unique method of forming a circle through the repetition of wedge-shaped portions.

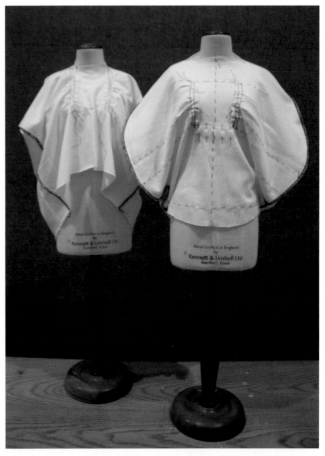

Fig. 6.16 Square and circle shapes can be draped on a half-scale mannequin, to provide inspiring starting points for the design process.

Fig. 6.17 This geometric garment toile has been created by modelling a rectangular piece of fabric on the stand. PHOTOGRAPHER: BOB SEAGO

Fig. 6.18 When draped on the stand, a square of fabric can create volume with fluid lines. PHOTOGRAPHER: BOB SEAGO

Zero waste

An important issue in terms of sustainability in the fashion and textiles industry is waste. The construction of fully fashioned knitwear is an inherently materially efficient process; because the pieces are knitted to shape, very little waste is created. Seamless construction is even more efficient. Yet, when conventionally shaped pattern pieces are cut from panels or continuous fabric, whether for knitwear or woven garments, waste is generated. Zero-waste pattern cutting addresses this inefficiency, by developing designs that use every part of the cloth through inventive cutting and construction. This method of making clothes can be a good choice for knitwear designers, whose main focus may be on the intricate stitches, texture and colour of the garment design. The pattern pieces are often large and without body shaping, allowing maximum opportunity to display the knitting techniques. Knitting also provides the opportunity to integrate slashes and holes into a piece as it is made, opening up the options available for construction.

Zero waste is not a new concept; the first garments were full animal skins draped over the body, followed by more intricate garments made from multiple skins that were sewn together. Some traditional garments, such as the ancient Greek chiton and Indian sari, use simple lengths of cloth; others, such as Chinese trousers made from rectangles, result from the cloth being split into geometric shapes that are joined together to create forms that can be worn on the body. Two designers who take inspiration from these simple forms of clothing and explore contemporary approaches to zero-waste pattern cutting are Timo Rissanen and Holly McQuillan. Many of their designs have started from the pattern shapes of the Japanese kimono.

Fig. 6.19 Multiple triangles of fabric that are seamed together can produce an unconventional yet relaxed silhouette.

PHOTOGRAPHER: BOB SEAGO

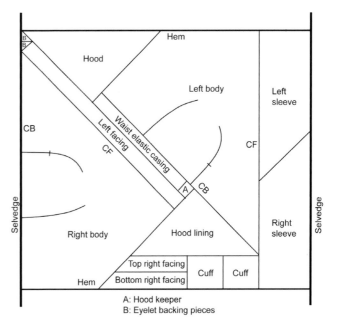

A: Hood keeper
B: Eyelet backing pieces

Fig. 6.20 This zero-waste hooded-top pattern, designed by Timo Rissanen, uses every part of the fabric.

Fig. 6.21 The unusual construction of the zero-waste hooded top, designed by Timo Rissanen, is emphasized by the striped fabric.

CHAPTER 7

CONSTRUCTION AND MANUFACTURING

by Helen Hill

Introduction

The distinctiveness of knitwear lies not only in its unique structure but also in its construction. Many of the processes that are used to make knitted garments are quite different to those that are used for items made from woven fabrics, because of the knitted structure's inherent characteristics. For example, consideration must be given to the stretch and flexibility of the fabric throughout the manufacturing process. Specialist techniques, skills and machinery are needed at every stage, from the first pressing of the knitted panels through to the addition of trims to the completed garment. A good knitwear designer will think carefully about construction throughout the design process, in order to develop a solution that fits the brief and their concept.

Knitted-garment manufacture varies dramatically in terms of scale, from the production of one-off, bespoke pieces to the volume production that is used by high street brands. It varies, too, in terms of location; while pockets of the traditional industry remain in areas of the UK, the vast majority of large-scale manufacturing now takes place overseas. Designers, therefore, may be working thousands of miles from the factories that will knit and construct their designs. Efficient processes are required to manage sampling and production in this global system. Whatever the scale or location, the manufacturer must work hard to ensure that they can fulfil the designer's vision, while producing a garment that is fit for purpose.

Key principles

In order to make confident decisions about construction, a knitwear designer must have a good understanding of the different ways in which knitted garments can be put together. The method of construction will inform both the way that a garment is knitted and the machinery that is used for make-up. The designer should also be aware of the contexts in which their designs might be manufactured and the important issues surrounding the complex supply chains being used in today's industry.

Linking is a unique manufacturing process that is used for the construction of knitwear garments. Learning this process provides the designer with a deeper understanding of construction possibilities.

Fig. 7.1   The Albion Knitting Company, established in north London in 2014, produces fully fashioned knitwear for high-end luxury brands. PHOTOGRAPHER: JOANNA BRAY

Fig. 7.2   The neckline on a fully fashioned garment is often cut by hand by using a pattern template. Once the neckline has been cut, a trim will be attached by linking. COURTESY: JOHN SMEDLEY LTD

Fig. 7.3   An overlocked seam, as shown here, can be easily distinguished from a cup seam or linked seam. This seam is formed from a three-thread overlock stitch.

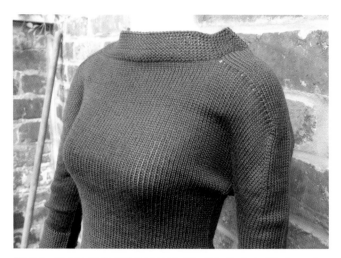

Fig. 7.4   Dr Jane Taylor's PhD research, titled 'The Technical Designer: A new craft approach for creating seamless knitwear', explored the design and development of innovative seamless-garment designs for the high street fashion market.

Manufacturing methods

Three methods are used to manufacture machine-knitted garments: fully fashioned, cut-and-sew and seamless. For fully fashioned knitwear, each garment panel is knitted to the desired size and shape; these shaped pieces are then assembled by using the specialist processes of cup seaming or linking. Although the overall aim is that the garment can be constructed without the cutting of any fabric, it is usual for the neckline to be cut and a trim – such as a rib or collar – to be attached by linking. Fully fashioned manufacture is seen as a high-quality method, and it is used by both high street companies and luxury brands. It has the benefit of producing little waste.

For the cut-and-sew technique, fabric is knitted, and then the garment pieces are cut out and assembled by using overlock machines. These may be garment-sized blanks knitted to specific widths and lengths with an integral welt (hem) and cuff, which are then cut using a pattern. Alternatively, continuous lengths of fabric can be produced, from which pieces are cut using a lay plan, in a similar way to the approach used for working with woven fabrics. Again, the garment is assembled by using overlocking; separate trims must be attached at the hem and cuffs. Cut-and-sew production is a fast method of knitwear construction, usually associated with garments for the large-volume and low-cost market level. However, if trims are attached by linking, use of this production method can be appropriate for garments associated with a high-end market level.

Seamless-garment manufacture has emerged through innovation in knitting technology, with flatbed machines now being able to knit a garment as a complete three-dimensional form. No make-up is required to assemble the garment, although a neck trim will usually need to be attached by linking. With the entire item being produced in a single process, seamless production is seen as a more sustainable approach to manufacturing knitwear – especially in comparison with cut-and-sew production, which generates waste fabric through the cutting out of necklines and sleeves. The lack of waste makes this method well suited for use with yarns made from expensive fibres and is typically used for luxury market levels. As discussed in Chapter 4, both circular- and warp-knitting technologies can also be used to create garments with a degree of seamlessness; however, in these cases, some cutting and sewing is typically still required.

While the general principles of manufacturing hand-knitted items are the same as those of manufacturing mass-produced, machine-knitted items, there are some distinctive differences. Pieces are typically made with minimal or no seams, and trims are often added during the knitting process. Where sewing is required, hand-sewing techniques are typically used; these processes are more time-consuming than those that use machinery.

Machinery

Some of the machinery that is used to manufacture knitwear can be found in any garment factory, such as overlock, lock-stitch, seam-cover and flatlock machines, along with machines for specialist processes such as the addition of buttonholes, buttons and bar tacks. The lock-stitch machine is frequently used for inserting zips and attaching components. Other machines – specifically the linker, mock linker and cup seamer – are unique to the construction of knitwear garments. The most widely used machines are the overlock machine, cup seamer and linker.

Used for the construction of cut-and-sew knitwear, the overlock machine simultaneously joins, trims and neatens in a single process. As the knitted fabric is fed through the machine, the blade cuts and trims a neat edge; the fabric is joined with either a three-thread or four-thread stitch formation, providing a secure seam that allows for the stretch of the fabric and encloses the raw edge. Adjusting the differential feed allows the machine to be adapted for different types and weights of knitted fabric. Overlocking is often labelled as a low-quality process, but this is partly due to the implementation of poor technique and the incorrect choice of yarns and threads.

Cup seaming is used in the manufacture of fully fashioned garments and produces a double-chain stitch, which is primarily

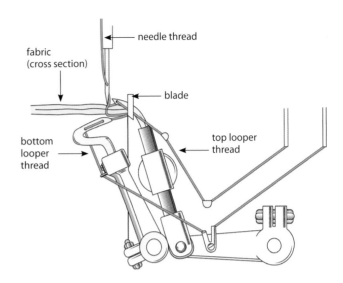

Fig. 7.5 A three-thread overlock machine is used to join cut-and-sew knitwear pieces. Three different sewing threads are used: cotton/polyester thread for the needle, bulk nylon thread for the bottom looper, and fine knitting yarn for the top looper. This provides a good-quality finish and coverage for the seam.

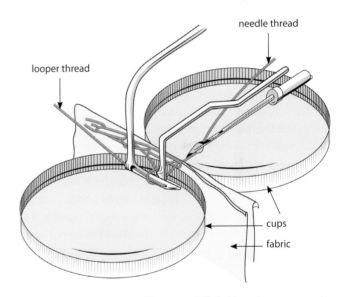

Fig. 7.6 Cup seaming is used for joining fully fashioned garment panels and produces a two-thread chain stitch. Two cups rotate to allow the fabric to be fed through the machine.

used for underarm and side seams. The machine consists of two counter rotating cups, through which the operator feeds the garment pieces, which are held in a vertical position. The stitch produced is elastic, making it ideal to accommodate the stretch of the knitwear. This process deals particularly well with the curling selvedge of single-jersey, fully fashioned fab-

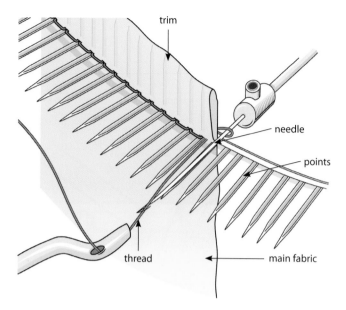

trim

needle

points

thread

main fabric

Fig. 7.7 Linking can be used for joining seams or attaching trims. The needle moves in a backward-and-forward motion, drawing the thread (actually a fine knitting yarn) from the looper to create a chain stitch.

ric. It produces a neat and durable seam, appropriate for a high-quality finish. Cup seaming is also used to temporarily join garment pieces when garments are to be washed, or wet finished, before being constructed. The cup seaming controls any fabric distortion occurring during the wet-finishing process and avoids the fabric becoming tangled; the chain stitch is easy to pull apart when the finishing process has been completed.

Linking is mainly associated with the manufacture of high-end, fully fashioned garments, as it provides a high-quality finish. The linker consists of a circle of curved points, protruding outwards from a rotating dial, and a moving needle that slides into each point in sequence. The linking stitch is a single chain, which has a degree of stretch and recovery. It should be noted that the stitch easily unravels if it is not securely fastened. Linking is used to attach all sorts of knitted trims to garments, such as for necks, strapping and pockets. It can also be used to create seams on fully fashioned garments, as an alternative to cup seaming. Linkers are available in different gauges, specified as points per inch on the circumference of the dial. A 10-point linker, for example, has ten points per inch. To link a seam, the fabric components must be assembled on to the points to meet a predetermined measurement before the components are stitched together. For some trims, such as neck sandwich trims, the positioning process involves sliding a single knitted

loop on to each point. Linking is a meticulous process that requires a high degree of skill and is well respected within the knitwear industry.

Manufacturing contexts

Knitwear manufacturing can take place on a small scale; manufacturing machinery can be acquired at a relatively low cost and used alongside domestic or hand-flat machines in a studio setup, to produce collections and one-off garments. As an alternative approach to small-scale production, advanced computerized flatbed machines can be used to produce customized knitwear garments that allow the consumer to be part of the design and manufacturing process. However, the vast majority of knitwear produced and worn today is mass-produced in a factory environment, whether in the UK or overseas. In this context, the garment will progress from one department to the next, from knitting through to finishing. Depending on the required quantity and quality of garments, production can be organized in different ways. For smaller orders, a single operative may produce an entire garment, while, for larger orders, a production line with multiple operatives, each specializing in a single process, may be used, in order to maximize efficiency.

Today, China is the largest global producer of knitwear. Investment in skills, technology and infrastructure has enabled Chinese suppliers to produce and export mass-market garments, as well as more exclusive items, including hand-knitted and embellished knitwear. Many businesses have head offices and factories in cities such as Hong Kong, Shanghai and Beijing, along with spinning plants and manufacturing units within the provinces. Other countries also have capacity for knitwear manufacturing; Bangladesh, for example, is known for manufacturing knitwear garments at a low cost for high street, volume brands. Many Bangladeshi garment factories have their own dyeing and finishing facilities, and the required yarn is easily sourced from local companies. In Europe, high-end, fine-gauge knitwear is made in Italy, while factories in Romania, Bulgaria and Turkey manufacture knitted outerwear, such as sweaters and cardigans, for high street brands. British knitwear manufacturing covers a variety of qualities and price points. Traditional high-end knitwear is still manufactured by a small number of long-standing companies, mainly in the Scottish Borders. Other factories produce either low-cost, cut-and-sew garments or small orders of high-quality knitwear, which are made by using fully fashioned and seamless techniques.

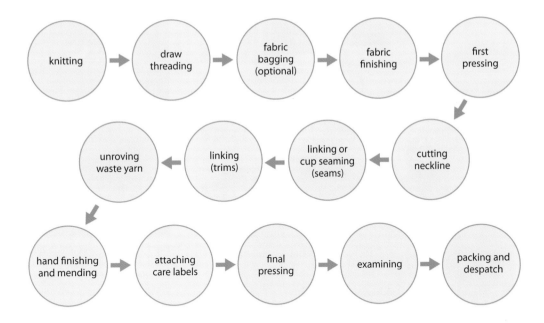

Fig. 7.8 The commercial production of knitwear requires careful planning and organization; delivery deadlines are critical for achieving maximum sales. This flow chart shows the manufacturing processes at each stage of production.

knitting → draw threading → fabric bagging (optional) → fabric finishing → first pressing

cutting neckline ← linking or cup seaming (seams) ← linking (trims) ← unroving waste yarn

hand finishing and mending → attaching care labels → final pressing → examining → packing and despatch

Fig. 7.9 The product-development or design office within a knitwear factory is typically a room partitioned off from the factory floor.
PHOTOGRAPHER: CHARLOTTE CAMERON

There are advantages to this global spread of manufacturing facilities: orders can be divided between different factories to make the best use of specialist skills and resources and to meet tight delivery deadlines. However, the system also brings major challenges. When product-development teams are geographically distant from the factories that they work with, knowledge of manufacturing processes is easily lost. Furthermore, a fragmented supply chain is difficult to monitor in terms of quality and employment practices. Awareness is increasing of the issue of workers' rights in the fashion industry, particularly since the

Rana Plaza disaster in Bangladesh in April 2013. A total of 1,134 people lost their lives when a building that housed several garment factories supplying high street retailers collapsed. In response to this tragedy, there has been a drive for transparency across the industry, with customers demanding information about the provenance of their garments, from the fibre used through to the finished item. These concerns are also encouraging interest in local and small-scale production.

Constructing a garment

Garment construction is the final stage of the design process, when the two-dimensional design becomes a realized three-dimensional outcome. In this section, we will work through the various stages of construction. While the principles apply to industrial production, we will be primarily thinking here in terms of a sample garment being produced for a micro-scale business or student collection.

Designing for manufacture

Planning for how to construct a garment is an important, though easily overlooked, part of the design process. The most fundamental consideration is whether the garment will use fully fashioned, cut-and-sew or seamless construction. Building on this decision, ideas for how to realize the design in three dimen-

Fig. 7.11 To achieve a high-quality finish when making a knitwear garment, the most appropriate type of manufacturing needs to be considered. This pocket, designed by Eleanor Drane, demonstrates the designer's high level of attention to detail.

Fig. 7.10 Knitwear students are taught garment-manufacturing skills. These pieces are part of a showcase of knitwear garments that were produced by students studying the BA (Hons) Fashion Knitwear Design and Knitted Textiles course at Nottingham Trent University.
DESIGNER: ROWAN CALVERT

Fig. 7.12 Flatlocking, as shown here, can give a sporty look to fashion knitwear garments.

sions should be generated during fabric sampling and garment design development. The selection of appropriate make-up methods should be informed by the brief and your research, in much the same way that decisions are made about yarn type, machine gauge, colour palette and so on. For example, to correspond to a sportswear-focused design concept, flatlocking might be used on top of the seams. Construction techniques and trim finishes, particularly those that are innovative or unconventional, should be sampled, evaluated and refined.

Awareness of costs will inform the choice of manufacturing techniques, particularly when working to a commercial brief. For example, linking requires more time and skill, and is therefore more costly, than overlocking. Designers in industry will require prior knowledge of a factory's capabilities in terms of machine types and capacity, in order to ensure that the garments to be

sampled will be easily interpreted into production garments. With the support of a specialist garment technician or product developer, designers may be able to creatively explore make-up processes. However, working within tight cost parameters may limit the options for innovation.

Prototype development

Before you can make a sample garment, a toile (prototype) should be made, in order to test and refine the design silhouette, the fit and the construction methods. This toile is the next step following the shell-shape toile described in Chapter 6. The closer the toile is to the intended final garment, the more successful the actual final garment will be. Therefore, the fabric used should simulate the stretch, handle, weight, fibre composition and structure of your proposed final fabric. You might choose to cut the pattern pieces from continuous fabric, particularly if your final garment is to be made by using the cut-and-sew method. However, if your final garment is to be fully fashioned, it will be more beneficial to knit the toile panels to shape, in order to fully test the construction methods. Before starting to put the toile together, you should carefully plan the sequence of make-up procedures.

Once the toile has been completed, the silhouette, fit and construction should be reviewed. Further toiles or part toiles may be required to resolve any problems; any alterations to the make-up sequence should be recorded. You may need to make changes to the design for technical reasons, which could alter the intended garment aesthetics. In this situation, the design concept must be balanced with practical considerations. Having completed the toile, the final sample garment can be produced.

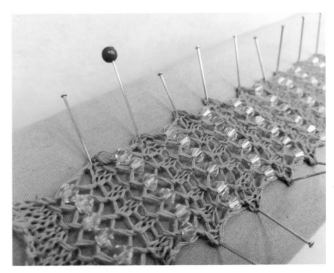

Fig. 7.13 Knitted fabrics require careful preparation before construction. Delicate knitted lace must be pinned and steamed, to eliminate the curl at the edges of the fabric. DESIGNER: JOANNA BRAY

First pressing and cutting out

Before starting to make up your garment, whatever the method of construction, the knitted fabric needs to be prepared via finishing and/or relaxation. A wet finish, used to remove the residual wool grease of the spinning process or to felt the fibres, involves washing the fabric in water with or without detergent or chemicals. A dry finish could include brushing or tumble-drying. Another form of preparation is relaxation of the fabric by using steam; through this process, the stitches tighten as the fibres settle into their new configuration in the knitted structure. Ideally, a flat steam bed will be used to ensure that equal amounts of steam are equally distributed throughout the garment. A steam iron can be used instead, but care must be taken to ensure that the garment is not overstretched and that the face of the iron does not touch the knitted fabric. The fabric is typically laid flat on to the bed for steaming, although some panels are stretched to a predetermined size by using a metal frame or by pinning into foam, to hold the fabric at the required dimensions. Hem ribs are not usually steamed, as they will lose all ability to recover. These preparatory steps are important: any relaxation or shrinkage after the garment has been constructed will result in the garment ending up being of the wrong size.

If cut-and-sew construction is being used, the pieces will need to be cut out by using shears (large scissors) and a pattern template. The fabric blank should be cut to the correct width, following the wale of the knitted fabric, before any curved or horizontal lines such as the neckline and armholes are drawn on and cut out. Fully fashioned and seamless knitwear would already have been shaped during the knitting process; however, it is common for the neckline to be cut out, rather than be knitted to shape. Again, it would be marked out and cut by using a template at this stage. If the garment has pockets or embellishment, these elements should be stitched before seaming, in order to allow the machinist to work on a flat fabric panel.

Seaming

Once the fabric has been knitted and shaped, whether through fully fashioned production or cutting, construction can commence. As described earlier, cut-and-sew construction will use overlocking, while fully fashioned construction will use cup seaming or linking. It is crucial to plan the order in which the seams will be joined, in order to maximize the sewing quality and the efficiency of production; this should have been decided at the toile stage. In order to ensure high-quality seams, the stitching should be tested and evaluated by using waste fabric. If you are overlocking, bear in mind that the fabric-handling technique for knitwear construction is different from that usually employed with woven fabric; because knit fabric is very stretchy, it is easily distorted when stitched.

Fig. 7.14 When overlocking knitted fabric, the fabric should be guided through the machine. Pulling or stretching of the fabric will cause distortion of the seams.

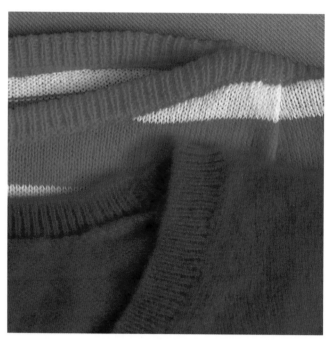

Fig. 7.15 These neck finishes demonstrate two different trims. The upper garment has a linked sandwich trim, which encloses the raw edges of the main-body fabric and produces a neat finish. The lower garment has a single-rib trim. It has been linked to the neck edge of the main body, which has been bound off and shaped rather than being cut.

The same sequence of assembly is generally applied to cut-and-sew knitwear garments and fully fashioned garments. For classic styles such as a crew-necked sweater with set-in sleeves, the shoulder seams are first stitched, with the incorporation of a woven tape to prevent the seam from stretching. Next, the sleeves are stitched to the flat body. The garment is completed by stitching from the hem in one operation, by joining the body sides and then the sleeve underarms with seams to complete the garment shell. If the sleeve head is curved, the sequence would be reversed. The sides and sleeve underarms would be joined, followed by working of a seam to join the sleeves to the body; this method is more sympathetic to the curved shapes being joined.

Attaching trims

Once the garment has been assembled, the trims can then be attached. These details are just as important as the silhouette, and the quality of the overall garment can be greatly enhanced by the addition of a carefully considered neckline and a beautiful finished edge. Trim requirements vary depending upon the design of the garment; for example, a sweater has a neck trim, while a V-neck cardigan has a continuous-opening trim known as a stole. Trousers and skirts each need a waistband. If the garment has raw edges on the sleeves and hem, these edges require cuffs and a welt trim, respectively.

Trims can be constructed in different ways. A single-thickness rib can be linked or overlocked, to create a neat and simple edging. Linked sandwich trims enclose raw edges to produce a neat finish and are typically used for necklines and cardigan

Fig. 7.16 This beautifully finished mitred V-neck trim, designed by Rowan Saunders, is constructed from a 2×2 rib and finishes with a short section of tubular single jersey. As for a sandwich trim, this tubular section encloses the cut edges of the main-body fabric.

Fig. 7.17 A strapping stole, knitted in a continuous strip, has been used to finish this cardigan opening. Seam cover stitch on the inside join covers the cut edge of the main body.

Fig. 7.18 A wire frame that has been electronically programmed with predetermined measurements allows a knitted garment to be stretched to the required size during its final press on a steam bed.
PHOTOGRAPHER: JOANNA BRAY

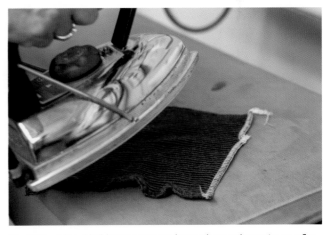

Fig. 7.19 A hand-held steam iron can be used as an alternative to a flat steam bed when making bespoke or sample garments.

stoles. The section of tubular knitted fabric that is included as part of other linked trims, such as a narrow rib, a polo neck or a collar, performs the same function. Knitted strapping is an alternative finish for a cardigan opening; whereas the length of a sandwich-trim stole would be restricted by the width of the needle bed, strapping can be knitted in a continuous strip. Trims should be joined only by using overlocking if the garment seams are overlocked. Linking creates a much more refined finish and is used for all types of construction, including that of seamless garments. Another approach is to knit trims, such as pockets and stoles, as an integral element of the garment.

Finishing and final pressing

Once the garment has been constructed, it is important to inspect it for faults. These could be fabric faults, such as holes or pulled threads, or seam faults, such as holes, broken sewing threads and missed linking. All loose threads should be neatly trimmed and secured.

The garment will require a final press, again to be performed on the steam bed. The garment is laid flat, with the sleeves nat-urally positioned. As with the previous press, ribs will typically be left off of the bed, in order to maintain their ability to stretch and recover. The steam is applied, and gentle manipulation of the seams and garment shape is all that is required; too much handling will distort the fabric. While pressing the garment, any changes such as shrinkage or discolouration can be noted for future reference.

Linking a neck trim

These instructions guide you through the process of linking an open-ended tubular neck trim to the body of a garment; the two layers of the tubular trim enclose the cut neck edge on the body. The example presented here is for the construction of a rib jumper with polo neck, but the principles can be adapted for other neck trims. The trim is usually calculated for a 58cm (23in) neck stretch, to allow the garment and its attached neck trim to fit over the head. The number of stitches of the edge of the trim to be linked to the garment should exactly match the number of points over this measurement on the linker, so that one stitch can be hooked on to each point. This can be easily calculated because linkers are identified by the number of points per inch. A trim to be linked on a 10-point linker would be 230 stitches wide (23in × 10 points per inch). A test swatch will establish which linker is most appropriate for the weight of fabric being used for the garment.

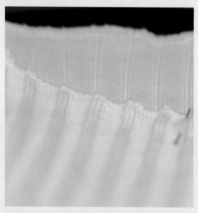

Fig. 7.20   Step 1.
Overlock the cut neck edge on the body of the garment, if the fabric is expected to fray. Mark on the neck edge the centre front, the centre back and the position that is 2.5cm (1in) towards the back from the left shoulder, to allow the neck-trim seam to sit slightly towards the back of the neckline.

Fig. 7.21   Step 2.
Use the markers on the linker dial to mark 10cm (4in) from the neck-trim seam to the centre back, 12.5cm (5in) to the right shoulder seam, 16.5cm (6.5in) to the centre front, 16.5cm (6.5in) to the left shoulder seam, and 2.5cm (1in) to the neck-trim seam. This allows for an even distribution of the trim to the body.

Fig. 7.22   Step 3.
Position the trim above the points of the linker, stretching the trim between the first and last markers on the linking dial. Push the trim on to the machine by hooking individual purl-side loops (shaped as a teardrop) of the open-ended tubular section on to each point, ensuring that each stitch is pushed fully on to the corresponding point.

Fig. 7.23 Step 4.
Push the body fabric on to the points, matching the measured marks on the linking dial to the marks on the neck edge. Ensure that the body fabric is evenly distributed by using the overlock stitches as a guide; the edges of the overlock stitches should sit slightly above the points.

Fig. 7.24 Step 5.
Fold the trim over, and push it on to the points by hooking individual knit-side loops (shaped as a V) on to each point, ensuring that each stitch is pushed fully on to the corresponding point. The last row of the trim will have been knitted as a slack course, allowing the stitches to easily fit on to the points.

Fig. 7.25 Step 6.
Once the trim- and body-fabric stitches are hooked on to the points to as far as the fabric stretch will allow, switch on the machine, and stitch the trim to the fabric. Once this section is stitched, gently pull the linked section off of the points, to allow the next section of stitches of the trim and body fabric to be hooked on.

Fig. 7.26 Step 7.
Continue stitching until the whole trim has been attached. Gently remove the garment from the linker, and secure the chain stitch by pulling the end of the linking thread through the last loop of the chain.

Fig. 7.27 Step 8.
Waste yarn is knitted on the end of the trim in a contrast colour of yarn to define the slack course. Once the neck trim has been stitched to the garment, the waste yarn is unroved (pulled back to unravel the stitches, row by row).

Fig. 7.28 Step 9.
The final process is to join the two open edges of the neck trim together by forming a seam, either by linking by machine or by sewing by hand. If sewing by hand, the edges of the trim are drawn together by using yarn matching the trim, to form a neat join.

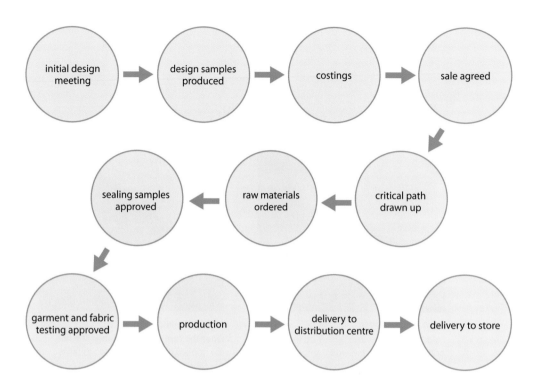

Fig. 7.29 The design development, manufacturing and delivery of knitted garments are managed through various stages of quality agreement and assurance between the supplier and the retailer.

Sampling and costing

Having established key principles of knitted-garment construction, we will now focus on the industrial context, to examine the processes, including costing, involved in taking a commercial garment from two-dimensional design to approved pre-production sample. These processes are typically supported by specification sheets, which document all aspects of the garment's design and technical construction.

Design sampling

The first sample to be produced in an industrial setting is the initial design sample, which will be used by the retail buyer for selection and range planning. In the context of a high-volume high street retailer, this sample will usually be made in one of the overseas factories that the company uses to produce bulk orders. The designer produces a tech pack, as discussed in a following section, to communicate their design requirements. It is important that these requirements are recorded accurately, as manufacturers will follow the garment flat, measurements and instructions exactly. Any errors will necessitate further sampling, which will slow down the process and add to the cost. Further samples may also be required if changes are made; for example,

if costing indicates that the initial design costs too much then the sample may be remade in an alternative yarn.

The challenges of long-distance sampling have led to some companies setting up their own design centres, to allow designers and technicians to work collaboratively and resolve designs more efficiently; this process is discussed in Chapter 4. An alternative is to use an independent design centre that provides a local design-development and sampling service for textiles and garments. A more innovative solution is to eliminate some physical sampling by using Shima Seiki's SDS-ONE APEX3 system to produce virtual three-dimensional samples. While some physical sampling will still be required for the assessment of handle and aesthetic, virtual sampling can be both cost-effective and efficient in terms of resource use and time.

Pre-production sampling

Once an order has been placed and a contract issued, the approved garment is handed over to the product-development team for the next stage of sampling and pre-production. This team must take the design sample and evaluate all aspects of its manufacture to ensure that it is fit for purpose: suitable for mass production and of an appropriate quality to be sold and worn. This process will involve establishing the most efficient

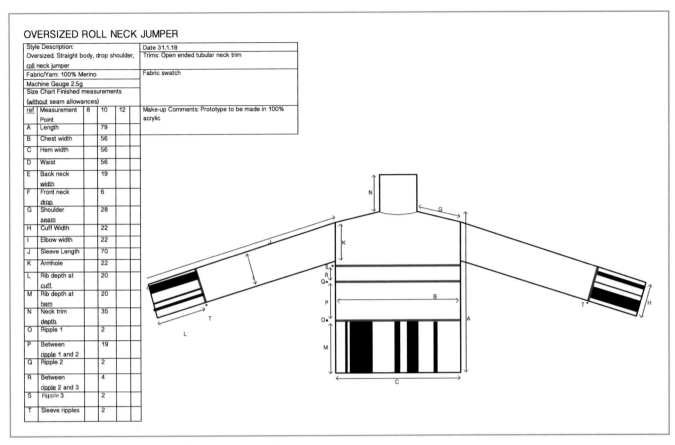

OVERSIZED ROLL NECK JUMPER

Style Description:				Date 31.1.18
Oversized. Straight body, drop shoulder, roll neck jumper				Trims: Open ended tubular neck trim
Fabric/Yarn: 100% Merino				Fabric swatch
Machine Gauge 2.5g				
Size Chart Finished measurements (without seam allowances)				

ref	Measurement Point	8	10	12	Make-up Comments: Prototype to be made in 100% acrylic
A	Length		79		
B	Chest width		56		
C	Hem width		56		
D	Waist		56		
E	Back neck width		19		
F	Front neck drop		6		
G	Shoulder seam		28		
H	Cuff Width		22		
I	Elbow width		22		
J	Sleeve Length		70		
K	Armhole		22		
L	Rib depth at cuff		20		
M	Rib depth at hem		20		
N	Neck trim depth		35		
O	Ripple 1		2		
P	Between ripple 1 and 2		19		
Q	Ripple 2		2		
R	Between ripple 2 and 3		4		
S	Ripple 3		2		
T	Sleeve ripples		2		

Fig. 7.30 In industry, samples are typically created by using the designer's tech pack. This includes a garment flat, detailed size chart, and yarn and knitting requirements. DESIGNER: JESSICA BRAITHWAITE

Fig. 7.31 The skill of the designer is to ensure that the design of the garment is appropriate to the customer's requirements and also meets the target price point. DESIGNER: JESSICA BRAITHWAITE. PHOTOGRAPHER: PHOEBE BOWDIGE

method of construction and carrying out a risk assessment to identify any causes for concern in terms of either production or wear. The design will also be graded into the full size range, with consideration being made of the proportion and balance of any stripes or other design elements within the knitted structure at each size.

Several pre-production, or 'sealing', samples are produced in the course of this process; each one must be approved, or sealed, by the buyer before the process can move on to the next stage. The samples then serve as a reference for both buyer and supplier. The approved design sample is sealed for aesthetics, colour and fit, and is the benchmark for all further garment production. The product-development team produce a graded set of size samples; once these are sealed, a pre-production sample will be produced and approved. Other pre-production approvals include those for yarn-dyeing samples, wearer trials, and wash-performance tests and their associated certificates. Finally, a garment from the bulk-production run will be required for production approval. A critical path is used to ensure that the pre-production process is managed to meet the planned production delivery date. This will include critical dates for sealing approvals and deadlines for the delivery of yarn and other raw materials.

Specification sheets

Specification sheets, which document and communicate details of the design and its construction, are used throughout sampling and production. A tech pack, which includes a design specification sheet, is often used during the design-sampling process, while a technical specification sheet is generated as part of the pre-production-sampling process and used during production.

The tech pack is created by the designer and includes all of the information that is required for the factory to produce the design sample. The design specification sheet includes front and back garment flats, a chart indicating key measurements for the sample size, detailed information about the yarn and any other materials such as buttons or trims to be included on the garment, and details of the knitted fabric's gauge and structure. Also included in the tech pack are any other materials, diagrams or details that are needed to produce the sample, such as a swatch of fabric to be replicated or a graph of the stitch structure. During the process of creating the sample, amendments may be made to the design; these changes will be recorded within the tech pack.

Once approved, the tech pack is then handed on to the production team who develop the bulk order for manufacture. They use it to create a technical specification sheet, which is used, along with the pre-production sealing sample, in various departments of the factory. The technical-specification sheet includes technical information for knitting and garment manufacture, enabling the approved knitted fabric and garment design to be replicated in production. Knitting details include yarn type, count and shade; machine type and gauge; and information on fabric quality, such as the stitch density (number of wales and courses per 10cm) and stitch length (length of yarn over 100 needles), along with details of structure and pattern. Information for garment construction includes the make-up sequence, details of the machines and threads to be used, finishing requirements and label requirements. The technical specification sheet also includes a size chart with key garment measurements.

Costing

A crucial element of manufacturing, whatever the scale of business, is costing. This process involves assessing the overall costs of a proposed design and making adjustments to ensure that the design can be produced and sold at a profit. Although a formal costing will be undertaken at the design-sampling stage, the designer working to a commercial brief will have been thinking about costs throughout the design process, from market research through to decisions about yarns, structures, garment details and manufacturing methods. In a mass-production context, a retailer's merchandising team will set a target retail price for a particular style and from this target will calculate a target wholesale price. The supplier then produces a costing, to establish whether they are able to manufacture the garment at a profit within the target wholesale price. If the cost is higher than the target price, the supplier will need to negotiate with the retailer or propose changes to the garment design to reduce costs.

The supplier's costing is generated through the consideration and recording of costs associated with five key areas: time, raw materials, transportation, overheads and profit. A time-and-motion study is undertaken to calculate the length of time required to knit and construct a garment. As each make-up process is timed, the complexity of different operations is taken into account and used to calculate the final cost accurately. Raw-material costs include the cost of sewing threads, zips and buttons, along with that of the yarn, the cost of which is

Costing Sheet Style Number Style Name	Chunky jumper - toile		Designer Name Season Date	Jessica Rose Braithwaite AW 18/19 May 2018	Sketch
Fabric	Quality	Price per cone	Rating	Total cost of fabric used	
Yarn 1	100% acrylic 4 ply 500g-2000m	£10.95	1.7kg	£43.80	
Yarn 2	66% mohair, 30% nylon, 4% wool 1/10Nm 230g-2500m	£27.50	50g	£6.88	
			Total Cost	£50.68	
Components					
n/a			Total Cost	£0	
CMT Cost - estimate				£50.00	
			GRAND TOTAL COST	£100.68	
			Wholesale Markup x 2.2	£220.00	
			Retail Markup x 2.8	£600.00	

Fig. 7.32 The calculation of accurate costs by using a costing sheet, as demonstrated in this illustrated example by Jessica Braithwaite, is a crucial element of the sampling process.

calculated by weight. Transportation costs will depend on the distance from the factory to the retailer's distribution centres; customs charges may be incurred if the goods cross international borders. Along with the costs directly related to the items being produced, the supplier must include a contribution to overheads, such as factory utility costs, machine depreciation and management salaries. Finally, the supplier must ensure that the order generates some profit.

Small-scale, designer-knitwear labels must go through a similar costing process. The direct costs of manufacture, overheads and profit are combined to calculate a wholesale price; stores buying the garments to sell at retail then apply their own markup, which represents a significant proportion of the final retail price. For example, a designer may pay a small factory £60 per garment and sell those garments wholesale to a boutique at £120 per garment. The boutique would apply a markup factor of 2.8, to give a retail price of £336. The designer would make

£60 per garment, and the boutique would make £216 per garment; both figures must cover the designer's and boutique's overheads and profits.

The cost of making a garment will vary from factory to factory, depending on the global location of the factory, the skills required to produce the garment, and the factory's available capacity for manufacturing. High-volume manufacturing can lead to lower make-up costs, as the factory can be set up to produce one style for a longer period of time. The familiarity of the style allows for a more efficient manufacturing flow; the operatives will be confident with the fabric-handling and construction processes, and fewer changes in machine threading will be needed. Small production quantities are less efficient as a result of the unfamiliarity of the style and of the machine adjustments that are required.

Quality and care

When constructing a garment, it is important to consider the way in which it will perform over time. Physical issues, such as holes, pulls, shrinkage and pilling, often prompt people to discard knitted items that might otherwise have a longer useful life. This causes significant problems in terms of sustainability. Therefore, it is crucial that designers and product-development teams understand the ways in which such problems can be minimized.

Quality control

Quality control is a set of procedures that are used to ensure that the garments being manufactured meet required standards. As a first step, the expected quality, colour and size of the garment must be established via the pre-production sealing sample. The sample is then used, along with the technical specification sheet, as part of the factory's quality system to monitor the garments as they are manufactured. The first checks take place before knitting commences, to confirm that the yarn and other materials meet the required specification. During production,

garments must be checked carefully. This involves inspecting the fabric for knitted-fabric faults and checking the seams for sewing faults. A final garment inspection then takes place prior to the garments being delivered. This final check includes measuring the garment and checking the measurements against the size chart. Given the flexible nature of knitted fabric, a tolerance of 1cm–2cm (approximately ½in–¾in) is typically applied to these measurements.

In order to measure aspects of garment quality, textile testing is used. Standard performance tests set by the British Standards Institute are performed under controlled conditions by an accredited testing house or laboratory. Initial tests are carried out on the garment prototype prior to production; the results indicate whether the garment is fit for purpose and provide information for the care label. Further testing then takes place on the garments being manufactured, in order to ensure that the same quality is maintained. Tests cover fibre composition; aspects of fabric performance, such as shrinkage and pilling; aspects of construction performance, such as seam strength; and the performance of the garment after repeated washing. Because the cost of testing impacts the final garment cost, the number of tests will be limited.

Fig. 7.34 Brand labels are usually sewn into the centre of the back neck by using a lock-stitch machine. Care labels are generally stitched within the left side seam.
COURTESY: JACK MASTERS LTD

Labelling

Many of the textile tests carried out as part of the quality-control process relate to durability: how a garment will perform with wear over a period of time. While this performance depends on the way in which the item is manufactured, it is also shaped by the way in which it is washed. Care labels provide guidance to the customer and are a legal requirement in the UK. Labels must include care instructions for either washing or dry-cleaning and details of fibre composition; optional information includes the garment size and the country of manufacture.

Care labels communicate instructions via symbols, which are contained within an International Standard: ISO 3758. This standard is written and maintained by a group of washing and labelling experts who meet regularly to ensure that the symbols reflect consumer practice across the world. Symbols indicate, for example, whether a product should be washed by hand or machine and at what temperature, whether it can be tumble-dried, and what temperature is appropriate for ironing the product. Some knitwear garments can be dry-cleaned; in this case, instructions must state the type of solvent to be used. If there are any obvious dangers associated with the care or use of the item, such as dye from a coloured garment running into other items in the wash, the label must contain a clear warning to this effect.

It is a legal requirement to state the correct fibre composition on the garment label. While this is straightforward for garments that are made from a single fibre type, it can be complex when multiple yarns made from different fibres have been used. In order to establish accurate percentages for each fibre, the garment will be unroved and the yarns weighed. This process is often carried out by an accredited testing laboratory.

Care and repair

Labels provide advice on garment care, but the understanding and skill of the consumer is needed in order to keep an item in use over a prolonged period of time. Knitwear is susceptible to a range of issues including pilling, pulling of stitches, fabric thinning and seam damage. Some problems may be linked to the characteristics of a particular fibre or yarn; some will be due to poor-quality construction processes, while others will be caused by accidental damage or a lack of care in terms of washing and drying procedures. For example, a knitted garment may shrink, if the temperature of the washing water is too hot, or stretch, if it is hung to dry rather than be laid flat.

Retailers and other organizations can help consumers to avoid or overcome these problems. Support may focus on increasing consumer awareness of how to properly care for a knitted garment or may relate to repair, through the provision of either professional services or instructional information. However, domestic-mending practices have declined in recent decades, and levels of skill are generally low. The specialist nature of the knitted structure can further deter wearers from attempting garment repairs; there is much scope for the development of such skills within the community, and this can be an important, though unconventional, challenge for the knitwear designer to address.

CHAPTER 8

CAREERS

by Ian McInnes

Introduction

Fashion knitwear is often perceived to be a niche specialism and, therefore, quite limited in terms of career opportunities. However, in reality, the discipline provides varied and diverse employment prospects, be they local or global. The education and training of a fashion knitwear designer provides an opportunity to explore both the knitted fabric and its development into a garment. Successful graduates in the subject are sought after; their expertise enables them to work across both the textile and the garment or product areas of the industry, from initial design idea through to its realization. Their knowledge of the industry can be readily transferred to broader fashion and textiles professional roles, including the sustainability-related roles that are gaining in importance, as companies seek to address their environmental and social impacts and even explore alternative business models. Furthermore, this breadth of expertise is transferable across textile applications, providing opportunities to move beyond the fashion sector.

Exhibiting your designs at the end of an undergraduate or postgraduate course is an important opportunity to promote your design skills and network with potential employers or clients. The styling of your garments in a static exhibition, catwalk presentation or photo shoot should link back to your design concept. This MA exhibition stand by designer Merina Pelander showcases her gender-neutral collection.

This chapter looks at the career opportunities within the fashion knitwear industry. It describes various roles, considering the main activities undertaken and key skills required. These roles span a range of contexts: designing for established brands, whether high street or luxury and whether in-house or via supplier companies; working independently by designing swatches, working freelance, setting up an independent label or designing hand-knitting patterns; and following alternative routes, including trend forecasting, teaching and academic research. Case studies gathered from professionals across the industry provide valuable insights into potential career paths, along with advice for young designers.

Designing for established brands

Many designers take up roles working for established brands, such as high street retailers and luxury labels. While in-house designers work directly for these brands, there are also opportunities to work for the manufacturing companies that supply them. Product development is a complementary role that is well suited to designers with strong technical skills. An alternative route is to work for a knitting-machine manufacturer, producing designs to showcase the capabilities of the technology to suppliers and brands.

In-house designer

Designers working directly in the head offices of brands and retailers develop main-line ranges and special collections for manufacture. Depending on the scale of the business, this may be a sole-designer role or working as part of a team of designers with varying levels of experience. The design department typically works in collaboration with other teams, such as those of merchandising, marketing and sales. Designers must have a good understanding of the company's critical path, which guides designs through the sampling and approval process described in Chapter 7.

Designers working for high street brands are normally concerned with volume production, designing to agreed price points, set product types and the manufacturing capacities of external suppliers. The design approach is guided by an understanding of the company's customer base, often identified through analysis of sales data from previous seasons, combined with an awareness of relevant trends. Designers working for luxury brands find that their roles have a greater emphasis on innovation and visual impact; their directional designs are more likely to define new trends and must satisfy a loyal and discerning customer base. Manufacturing may take place within the company or be outsourced to suppliers of specialist processes and materials on a season-to-season basis.

Kate Bell, Senior Casualwear Designer, John Lewis plc

I have a BA degree in printed-textile design from Duncan of Jordanstone College of Art and an MA in knitted textiles with computer applications from the Scottish College of Textiles, now Heriot-Watt University. I was a knitwear designer at Johnstons of Elgin for six years and then freelanced for three years with Marks & Spencer, which led to a full-time role. After three years, I moved to my current employer. I started as a knit designer and now design multi-products and oversee John Lewis, And/Or and the Weekend womenswear ranges. I love the three-dimensional, tactile nature of knitting and the infinite variety of possibilities; the most dramatic changes can come by simply changing yarn or gauge. A typical day starts with replying to emails from the global supply base. Overseeing three ranges means I touch base with each team to discuss any issues or ideas; the buying team provide a daily progress update. Problem solving is the main focus. With twenty years' experience, I bring a sense of perspective to the job: I see the bigger picture and don't overreact if something goes wrong. The best part of my job is seeing the junior members of my team develop, and their excitement when their designs go into store. My advice to new designers is to ask questions, be truthful and remember that you are usually part of a team, so don't let ego derail you. It is vital to see things from both sides – as a designer and as a manufacturer – and be able to negotiate between the two. And always be kind: it's a small world. An interview portfolio should be clear in its layout and showcase the variety of your skills and knowledge. Use fashion sketches to show how knit pieces might work with wovens as a total fashion collection. Research the company: visit their stores and websites, look closely at the pieces they offer, and consider how you could add to that and develop it further. Create a small personal project around this, to show that you are prepared to work hard to get the job.

CASE STUDY

Pip Jenkins, Head Designer, John Smedley Ltd

I studied textiles at college before going on to study a degree in fashion design at Kingston University. I became frustrated at never finding the right fabric for my designs; in developing my own fabric, I found my passion for knitwear. It was rewarding and exciting to design and produce every aspect of the garment myself and create the vision I wanted to achieve. While studying, I was a design assistant at Richard Nicoll and Sibling; I also worked for Brooks Brothers in New York after winning an industry-based project. These experiences helped me to develop specific skills and to understand where I saw myself after graduating. In 2009, I was selected as the Best of British knitwear designer by *Vogue Italia* and showcased my portfolio at Milan Fashion Week.

I've been in my current role since 2013. I oversee all aspects of design for menswear, womenswear and special projects, from concept to production and promotion. I am able to look at the synergy of a design: how the texture, shape and colour all add to the overall look of a garment. We are currently in the development stage of the next collection: building spec packs, knitting new textures and patterns, colouring up the collection, working with production on price point and quality, and ordering the new yarns ready for sampling. It is great to see the final samples being crafted by experts – and the campaign shoot, which launches every new collection in showrooms around the world. Administration, although less exciting, has to be done. Information must be communicated correctly for the collection to go through each process point without hiccups.

My advice to new designers is to make the interview portfolio as tactile as possible; touch is so important in the knitwear industry.

Fig. 8.1 The John Smedley design studio is based in the company's factory, which allows Head Designer Pip Jenkins to see the designs at every stage of development. COURTESY: JOHN SMEDLEY LTD

Sketching and professional CAD designs are vital. A mix of projects shows that you can be flexible and adapt to a brand's vision and aesthetic.

Stacey Tester, Design Director of Knitwear and Jerseywear, Marc Jacobs

As part of my degree course in fashion knitwear design at Nottingham Trent University, I undertook a work placement in New York; after graduating, I moved there to work at TSE Cashmere. The technical knowledge that I learnt in my degree suddenly made sense when I needed it in the real world. For the first two years, I focused on research and development. I was then given creative responsibility for the contemporary line tseSAY, developing the collection from concept through to final presentation. After three years, I moved to Ralph Lauren. For seven years, I was the senior design director of the women's knitwear collection, mentoring a large team who worked on the luxury categories for the brand and working with Ralph Lauren on the runway knitwear. I love the intense energy of elaborate runway presentations. There is always a new challenge, and this drives me creatively.

At the beginning of each season, I spend a lot of time brainstorming ideas and researching materials, garments and imagery. We travel once or twice per season to work directly with our overseas suppliers in Asia and Italy. I mentor a team of junior designers, and we start the day discussing the work flow and setting timelines. I also spend a lot of time communicating with merchandising, sales and design. Remaining focused and solving complex and varied problems in a highly pressured environment is crucial. Developing product that fulfils creative requests but also meets business needs and stays within price-point goals is one of the more challenging, but most necessary, parts of my job.

I still have so much to learn; I stay connected and open to new developments within the industry. The global knitwear industry is very small, and there is a lot of support for one another. Passion and inquisitiveness are something I look for when I hire young designers.

Fig. 8.2 Stacey Tester worked at TSE Cashmere and Ralph Lauren before moving to her current role as Design Director of Knitwear and Jerseywear at Marc Jacobs.

When I am interviewing, I prefer to see sketchbooks that illustrate a thought process and the development of an idea; I am much more interested in the journey, rather than just the end result. Working within a designer company, the ability to research and develop ideas is highly valued.

Other roles

Rather than working directly within the studios of established retailers, many designers work for the manufacturing companies that supply them. These suppliers speculatively develop and present ideas to retailers' buying teams from season to season. The designer must develop ideas to the price points and quality standards required by a particular retailer and manage their designs as they progress through the sampling and costing process, as described in Chapter 7.

A product developer typically interprets designers' ideas by using the materials and technology available, with consideration for quality, timelines and costs. It is vital for those working in this role to have an excellent understanding of the capabilities of materials, machinery and the skilled workforce; they also need an excellent grasp of technical terminology and the ability to communicate complex information.

With the development of digitally programmed knitting machines, a new role has emerged in which designers are employed by machine suppliers to develop fabrics and garments that are constructed by using the latest manufacturing technologies. The designers work in the sales showroom to demonstrate the creative possibilities of the machinery and software. These designers are hand-picked for their combination of design and technical know-how, their digital skills and their enthusiasm for the machinery and product capabilities.

Working independently

Some designers wish to work more independently; career paths of this type of designer include swatch design, free-lancing, launching an independent label and designing hand-knitting patterns.

Swatch designer

Swatch designers develop innovative and forward-looking knitted samples that are sold to retailers and brands. These swatches often provide fabric and garment-trim ideas in one design, by simulating a garment front or 'mini garment'. When a sample is purchased, the customer acquires the exclusive right to use the design in their collections. Designers may work as part of a team within a studio or on a freelance basis, selling via agents. While swatches have traditionally been produced on hand-flat or domestic machines, some swatch-design studios are now purchasing state-of-the-art digital manufacturing machines and design software programmes, enabling them to offer industry-ready samples for power production knitting.

Freelance

Freelance designers produce ranges for a portfolio of industrial clients. The work can be ad hoc and short term or can progressively accumulate and extend over a much longer period. Freelancers undertake activities such as developing new products for new markets and improving working methods, from sourcing through to design and sales. When working freelance, you must develop your profile and identify your unique selling point. What can you offer that an in-house knitwear specialist cannot? What differentiates you from other freelance designers? To gain a good reputation, it is important to be able to communicate well and have know-how and foresight.

Jennie Cox, Design Director, Bobble swatch-design studio

When studying a degree in fashion, I found that using another designer's fabrics wasn't stimulating enough for me. We had machine-knitting sessions, and I immediately knew this was the direction for me. I went on to study a degree in fashion textiles with business administration, specializing in knitwear, at what is now the University of Brighton. After graduation, I freelanced for leading knit-swatch studios in London, then travelled to New York and decided that, if I could get a position in knitwear design, I would stay. I secured a job in three days with a leading US label. It was an amazing role with huge responsibility, where I was exposed to production as well as design work and sales teams. I then launched Bobble in New York in 2001. I had been getting frustrated with the constraints of working for a corporate company and feeling less creative. In 2003, I returned to the UK, and Bobble found its home in Brighton.

In the studio, I work on a digital power knitting machine, which is creatively addictive. Bobble clients receive the full digital knitting programme of each design and therefore know that our designs can be manufactured. Working from the USA with factories in Korea, China and Hong Kong gave me invaluable experience when designing for manufacture. My work also involves administration, chasing payment, ordering yarns and providing factories with instruction and direction. When I'm not in the studio, I'm visiting clients globally: from Karl Lagerfeld's atelier in Paris to the Tommy Hilfiger head office in New York. The Pitti Filati trade show in Florence is my favourite trip on the calendar.

My advice to new designers is to be passionate and love what you do. Be prepared for a lot of hard work and knock-backs, and learn about technology for the future as well as today. A graduate portfolio should show personality. A knowledge of industry and an interest in leading designers must come through, along with an ability to create trend boards and shop reports. The use of digital technology in the design and communication of ideas is vital.

Carola Leegwater and Eva de Laat, Studio Eva x Carola

We met as students of technical and commercial clothing sciences at the Amsterdam Fashion Institute in 1998, and then together in 2001 we took up internships at Tunji Dada Studios in New York, working on material developments with alternative craft manipulation techniques. In 2004, we were employed by Nike in Amsterdam to develop products for professional sports applications to enhance performance. In 2010, Eva moved to Shanghai and Carola moved to London, to work independently, and then in 2014 we collaborated with circular-machine supplier Santoni, to develop seamless technologies and products. Being influenced by different cultures and ways of living, we combine our conceptual ideas and creative direction with Santoni's technical knowledge, resulting in new ways of knitting.

As we work across different time zones, our way of working is nomadic. Eva works closely with Santoni, based in Shanghai. Each morning, there is an update across the expert team of technical engineers on progress with new experiments and design direction. We work directly with the specialist machines and technicians and communicate and discuss our various projects, test results and next steps. Access to advanced digital technology is paramount to us in generating a three-dimensional product, by tailoring yarn and machine settings stitch by stitch. We are in constant dialogue with each other and our clients via our mobile phones on WeChat, Skype and email. Although administration takes us away from our love of knitting, it helps us to analyse our work, push ourselves forward as a team and do the job well.

Young designers need to develop an experimental approach and convert opportunities into actions wherever possible. The ability to communicate with many cultures, backgrounds and personalities is an advantage. Learning comes from early failures. Trust in yourself: show your unique self, not a replication of today's social-media world. It is better to dream than not to dream at all.

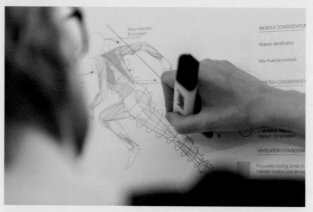

Fig. 8.3 Carola Leegwater and Eva de Laat work in close collaboration with the seamless-circular-machine manufacturer Santoni, combining their own conceptual ideas and creative direction with the company's technical knowledge.

Fig. 8.4 Studio Eva x Carola combines a mathematical approach with creative design and body-mapping, for the design of functional seamless knitwear.

CASE STUDY

Jo Bee, Freelance Knitwear Designer and Visiting Lecturer

Fig. 8.6 The design for this chevron-lace swatch by freelance designer Jo Bee was inspired by the patterns and textures of Marrakesh.

Fig. 8.5 The SpinExpo trade fair is one of freelance designer Jo Bee's regular clients. This catsuit mixes delicate lace stitches with open crochet strips that contour the body.

What drew me into knitwear is its versatility. Through gauge and yarn choices, you can create something really slick or something really textural and sculptural. I took a placement at a leading swatch company while studying for my fashion knitwear degree at Nottingham Trent University; knitting swatches every day allowed me to be increasingly experimental and creative. After university, I started an internship at Julien Macdonald as knitwear assistant, which led to a full-time job designing for the catwalk collections. I worked under the direction of Julien to design couture dresses for Beyoncé, Kim Kardashian and Gwen Stefani, and my work featured in *Vogue* and

Elle Wedding. After five years, I went freelance; I now have a portfolio of clients, from leading UK swatch studios to new high-end fashion labels, and I work regularly for the trend area at the leading trade fair SpinExpo. I also teach on fashion and textiles degree courses.

I love being creative and the diversity of working on different projects and with different people. While I love every stage of the design process, I don't love the admin, chasing invoices, tax returns, boxing things up, and doing post-office runs. Being freelance, it all falls to me. I keep focused on being relevant and innovative and advancing my knowledge and skill. For example, I have refined and pushed my expertise in fashioning for high-end luxury products.

A successful freelance designer has experience in different areas of the knitwear business and awareness of current issues across the industry. My advice to young designers is to be creative and experimental on your knitting machine: the possibilities are endless. The portfolio for your first job interviews should include knitted swatches to promote your technical versatility. Keep updating your CAD skills, and showcase these across your portfolio pages. Hand drawing is also important; many companies still do their design work by hand.

Independent-label roles

When a designer establishes their own independent label, they typically take ownership of the entire process, from sourcing materials and generating ideas through to marketing and sales, acting in multiple roles that are often grouped under the title of director. They may produce the products themselves or outsource the manufacturing of their range to a factory or skilled outworkers. While this path offers creative freedom, it also carries great responsibility and the need for a diverse skill set. Knowledge of your market is crucial; selling directly to individual customers via online platforms or at events offers the opportunity to test ideas and get immediate feedback.

CASE STUDY

Lachlan Munro, Director of Lachlan Munro Ltd and Studio Roam

I have a textile-design degree, specializing in knitted textiles, from the Scottish College of Textiles, now Heriot-Watt University. My first job was as assistant designer of felted textiles and products at Tait & Style in Orkney. I then studied for an MA in women's knitwear at the Royal College of Art. After setting up a knitwear-consultancy partnership named Brett Munro in the Scottish Borders, I established a micro knitwear factory to develop the brand Roam and focus on the design and production of bespoke knitted cashmere blankets. I now work as a lone studio designer-maker and also freelance as a factory designer.

A normal consultancy day starts with checking emails and catching up with programmers and the sample room on progress with new designs. The remainder of the day is spent liaising with the design studio, technical teams and sample room with updates and planning. At the Roam factory, I organize my activities through the week; these activities include finance and business planning; research, design and programming; website development and sales; and talking to existing and potential customers. The best part of my job is hearing customers' excitement if a development is just as they imagined – or even better than they imagined. Telling employees that something is incorrect and needs sorting very quickly is less enjoyable. The industry demands dedication and passion, a thick skin and strong people skills. You can be the most fantastic designer, but if you don't have good people skills you will rarely achieve what you want with a factory. In a graduate portfolio, I look for a strong personal identity, clear and concise presentation, variety and trend awareness.

Fig. 8.7 Lachlan Munro draws on his creative-design and technical-programming skills to produce personalized knitted cashmere blankets for his label Studio Roam.

Fig. 8.8 Lachlan Munro splits his time between working as a solo designer-maker and providing consultancy for larger brands.

Rory Longdon, Freelance Knitwear Designer and Creative Director

Fig. 8.9 Designer Rory Longdon has designed for brands including Max Mara, Belstaff, Mugler, Tory Burch and Ermanno Scervino.

Fig. 8.10 Rory Longdon and his business partner produce highly refined knitwear for their own label, as well as working on consultancy projects.

I knew I wanted to do fashion design, but then I discovered the knitting machine! The possibility to create both the textile and the finished garment really appealed to me. After graduating from Nottingham Trent University with a degree in fashion knitwear design and winning the Graduate Fashion Week Gold Award, I designed women's knitwear across three collection lines for the MaxMara fashion group in Italy. Two years later, I moved to Belstaff in New York to design women's and men's knitwear. I then returned to Italy, offering design consultancy to established brands such as Mugler, Tory Burch and Ermanno Scervino. I met my business partner, and together we work on our own collection and consultancy projects.

Knitwear is very technical, and it is essential to have a good grasp of this before starting to design. My education helped me develop this knowledge, along with the skill and confidence to push my creativity. A day in the studio is always different, from hand or power machine knitting swatches for a client to garment sketching for our own label or linking garment panels together. I most enjoy experimenting with the power knitting machine, but paperwork such as spreadsheets for yarn orders and making line sheets for garment sampling and production also need to be done each day.

I am focused, creative and technically strong. In my opinion, a good design portfolio should show creativity with stitch and technical know-how with yarn, structure and garment construction for real products. Learn and ask as much as you can, and take advantage of all the opportunities and experiences in industry that you can. If you find your current job isn't satisfying you then do personal or mini projects. They will always be helpful in demonstrating your capabilities to future employers.

Hand-knitting designer

While the majority of fashion knitwear designers work in the context of industrial production, another route is to generate designs to be produced by hobby knitters. Hand-knitting patterns are found in a range of contexts: in specialist magazines, in beautifully produced books, in single patterns produced by spinners of hand-knitting yarn and, increasingly, online. Patterns must be carefully checked before publishing, as any errors will cause problems for those attempting to use them. Pattern designers often complement their design work with related activities such as teaching workshops.

CASE STUDY

Debbie Bliss MBE, Head of Debbie Bliss at LoveCrafts

I studied fashion and textiles from 1970 to 1973 and then became a freelance hand-knitting designer. I was a PR for Hayfield Yarns for fifteen years and then knitting editor at *Woman's Weekly*. I also designed four collections of children's knits for Baby Gap. For over thirty years, I have produced books of hand-knitting designs with various publishers. In 2000, I launched my own brand of hand-knitting yarns and in 2016 was awarded an MBE in the Queen's Birthday Honours List for my contribution to the hand-knitting and craft industry. In 2018, after my distributor became insolvent, I sold my business to LoveCrafts, where I now work as head of the Debbie Bliss brand.

Two days a week, I go into the LoveCrafts offices in Holborn and meet up with the team, to discuss design briefs for future collections, yarn developments, and marketing and promotional activities. The rest of the week, I work in my studio in east London, working on the collections, researching ideas and knitting fabric swatches. There is so much I enjoy about my job. One of the highlights is a trip to Florence twice a year for the Pitti Filati trade show. I love the excitement of knitting a fabric swatch, when, after many attempts, one works and you can envisage the finished garment. I also enjoy the photo shoots, when months of work finally come together. I find the administrative side less exciting: keeping track of tasks and the nightmare of spreadsheets.

Although I have developed my knowledge over many years, I am always willing to learn new tricks, and I enjoy working with a young team. When I left college, I couldn't get a job, and I worked as a cleaner and in a factory; these experiences make me appreciate how lucky I am now to do a job I love. My advice to young designers is to treat people well and never be afraid of being nice. Put the most relevant work at the front of your portfolio and adapt it to the company you are seeing. Take notebooks or sketchpads to show the thought processes behind the portfolio: even unfinished work can be of interest.

Fig. 8.11 Hand-knitting designer Debbie Bliss has been awarded an MBE for her contribution to the hand-knitting and craft industry.

Karie Westermann, Hand-Knitting Designer, Tutor and Writer

I began knitting as a hobby, then within a year got a part-time job with a yarn company, providing designs to help them sell more yarn. I realized I had a knack for it. Five years later, I went freelance, publishing regularly in UK knitting magazines and selling patterns online. I teach, appear regularly in magazines and have just published a book. I like the storytelling element of hand knitting and the cerebral challenges of going from idea to finished pattern.

I don't sit around all day hand knitting! Every day is different: from writing emails to researching a new project, pitching to potential clients, pattern writing, creating marketing content or teaching. I have a part-time assistant who helps with paperwork and emails. I hand knit samples in the evening when I'm watching TV or with friends. I love researching in archives and museum collections and reading about a given topic. I recently designed and published a collection based upon Mesolithic archaeology and land art, and learnt about soil erosion and oil-exploration vessels in the process. It is gratifying to see people make something from my patterns and know that I've given them the tools to tell their own stories through their making.

Strong communication, technical pattern writing and conducting research are core skills in my current role. My own design work is self-directed and showcases my critical thinking, reflective design process, decision-making and flexibility. I work methodically from the idea stage to a fully realized pattern ready to purchase. While creativity is important, you also need to think about the practical and business implications. A willingness to attend meetings and to work with spreadsheets and specifications and to deadline will make your creative tasks possible.

Fig. 8.12   Karie Westermann, who started knitting as a hobby, is now a successful hand-knitting designer. Her patterns appear regularly in magazines; she also teaches knitting workshops and has published her own pattern book.

Alternative routes

Alternative career paths on offer to the fashion knitwear designer include trend forecasting, teaching and academic research.

Trend forecaster

The trend-forecasting role requires a deep awareness of the zeitgeist and the ability to anticipate cultural, social and economic influences on fashion and consumer behaviour, combined with an appreciation of the breadth of the market and the manufacturing and retail environment. It is important for forecasters to have the ability to generate inspiring imagery, to develop new themes and to generate or commission knitted fabrics that respond to these themes. The skills of communication and persuasion are vital; written, visual and verbal skills are needed to get the message over clearly and succinctly in publications, online and through live presentations.

Helen Palmer, Director of Materials, Textiles and Knitwear, WGSN

To me, knitting was the most difficult of the textile disciplines at college, and I could not keep a single piece of knitting on the machine for about three weeks. However, I mastered it, and I fell in love with the way that a garment can grow from a linear thread. After graduating from the University of Brighton, I moved to east London and split my time between knitting swatches and working as a theatre-costume maker. My first full-time job was in trend and product marketing for wool fibre, covering colour, yarn, knitwear and textile trends. Seven years later, I was asked by a Hong Kong-based, fast-fashion knitwear manufacturer to set up and run a knitwear design and trend studio in London.

Twelve years ago, I joined WGSN and transferred all of my trend and product-development know-how into a virtual, digital space. As Design Director, I contribute to creating and implementing content strategies, manage an editorial team, create content and have a public role delivering seminars, client presentations and bespoke consultancy projects. The best parts of the job are the variety of projects I work on and the pace of publishing. I am very fortunate to be working in a busy office brimming full of exceptional, talented, inquisitive and hard-working journalists, data scientists, designers and trend forecasters, all experts in their fields, talking and writing about things that excite and fascinate them. I love being able to 'join the dots' conceptually and visually between ideas or products in a way that feels new and makes a compelling story, communicated digitally through images and text. Being obsessively curious, I look at the world of art, design and culture, as well as keep myself informed on current affairs, consumer insights and the business marketplace, to help me see where the big shifts are coming from and how they might effect change.

My advice to young designers is to champion sustainability, as the fashion and textiles industry is due for a disruptive and radical transformation, and new opportunities, challenges and job roles will

Fig. 8.13   Helen Palmer, Director of Materials, Textiles and Knitwear at WGSN, brings a wealth of experience in trend forecasting and product development to her current role.

arise out of this challenge. We are in a buyer-driven, data-led world, where future designers will need to be multifaceted, business-minded and able to stand shoulder to shoulder with buyers. Always keep an open mind, keep learning and never get complacent.

CASE STUDY

Stephen Trigg, Creative Director, UPW

An interest in craft led me to study a degree in textile design at what is now the University of Brighton. I love knitted textiles for their creative potential in three dimensions and the fascination of what can be done with a simple knit, miss or tuck stitch. A masters degree from Nottingham Trent University led to my first job, heading up the creation of knitwear-trend publications at a leading fashion-forecasting house. After teaching knitwear in Scotland, where I instilled my passion for encouraging students' creativity, I took up roles at Marks & Spencer: first men's knitwear designer, then developing multi-product ranges and establishing the Collezione brand identity. I moved to a company manufacturing women's knitwear in Asia for the UK high street, being responsible for sourcing and designing yarns; that role developed my current specialism. The China-based spinner UPW employs me to design yarn collections and to create an identity for the brand that appeals to a global market. The challenge of balancing creativity and commerciality has enabled me to function in every one of these roles.

I have a voracious appetite for innovation. I am constantly updating my knowledge of fashion, textile and fibre trends through online professional networks, trend services and social-media platforms and checking in with international news stories to ensure I am up to speed with cultural and political issues, which may impact on consumer behaviours. I contact fibre suppliers to see what's new and liaise with marketing on advertising and exhibition design. Otherwise, my days are filled with meetings to progress yarn and fabric development and testing, production and costings. I put new

Fig. 8.14   Stephen Trigg's career has taken him from knitwear design and trend forecasting to designing yarn collections for a major spinner.

yarn ideas into work by finding ways to communicate the essence of what I want the yarn to achieve. I appreciate the needs of production but always question its limitations. Having such amazing resources at my fingertips is such a luxury that it never escapes me how lucky I am.

I think it is important to be humble and inquisitive. I have been creating a team to take over my role, and the driving forces behind my choices are enthusiasm and creativity; the rest can be learnt on the job. The portfolio needs to sparkle with creativity, individuality and originality and show a flow of ideas, not a timeline of projects in chronological order. Show who you are, what you are passionate about and that you have an opinion.

Teaching and academic research

While industry might be the most obvious context for the knitwear designer to work, academic settings also offer exciting and creative career opportunities. Teaching is one obvious route, whether teaching the specialism of knitwear on undergraduate or postgraduate courses, or more general art, design and textiles skills at GCSE, further-education or foundation level. Designers wishing to move into university teaching often start as a Visiting or Associate Lecturer, combining design tutorials or workshop-based sessions with independent design work.

Perhaps less obvious are the opportunities for knitwear designers to generate new knowledge by engaging in design-led academic research. Research can be undertaken at MA level or at a higher level of sophistication via an MPhil or PhD. Research also forms an important part of some university lecturers' roles or can be a full-time occupation. Research relating to knitting and knitwear is incredibly diverse; sustainability, smart textiles and heritage crafts are just a few of the topic areas that a research-focused knitwear designer might investigate.

Lucy Turner, Head of Quality and Validations and Principal Lecturer in Fashion Textiles, Oxford Brookes University

Fig. 8.15 Lucy Turner's MA, for which she studied alongside her teaching role, provided a setting in which to research the use of knitted textiles as a medium to raise awareness of the resurgence of tuberculosis.

After graduating with a degree in fashion knitwear design from Nottingham Trent University, I became a maternity designer at Dorothy Perkins but felt the job was limiting creatively, as ideas were compromised by cost and following trends. After freelancing, I bought a knit-swatch studio business and took frequent selling trips to design studios in New York and to trade shows in Florence

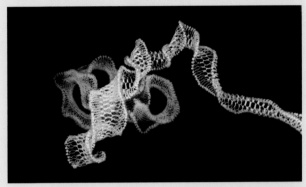

Fig. 8.16 Lucy Turner's MA project has opened up opportunities for further collaborative research.

and Paris. This left me with little time to design. I decided to do some teaching in 2009 and loved it. It was a free space to operate creatively, without the pressure of trends, costs and customer needs. I became course leader of a foundation art-and-design course in 2011 and moved to my new role in 2017.

A typical teaching day is tutorial-based, working in the studio with students on their design development and portfolios, and teaching processes and techniques. I also create bespoke project experiences, which stimulate a different way of thinking or a change in pace and productivity. The best part of teaching is thinking up new projects that will really challenge a student's idea of what fashion and textiles is and pushing students to respond as creatively as possible. I love helping them to lay out their most treasured work in portfolios. The least exciting task in teaching has to be organizing the timetable and booking rooms.

Don't see your career as a straight line from A to B. A willingness to undertake additional training or qualifications at relevant times in your life will enhance your career progression. Doing an MA as a mature student has meant I am more resilient, more focused and more capable of dealing with obstacles. I have the freedom in my MA research to investigate and delve into my research question, network with experts for comment and advice, and push my discipline so that others within the field are intrigued and impressed by what I have done. It has also opened up possibilities for more advanced collaborative research.

Dr Jane Scott, Senior Teaching Fellow, University of Leeds

Fig. 8.17 Dr Jane Scott spends considerable time programming, testing and documenting in connection with her environmentally responsive, experimental knitted textiles.

After a degree in textile design with French, I worked as a knitwear designer for a high street supplier, picking up CAD and garment-design skills while in the job. I moved on to accessories design before taking a university teaching post. I have always been interested in three-dimensional form, and as soon as I began working with knitting I could see the potential to generate unique forms directly from materials. My interest in architectural textiles first emerged through undertaking an MA in fashion and textiles. It then evolved into designing new material systems for environmentally responsive, smart textiles for architecture as a PhD at Central Saint Martins College of Art and Design. My work aims to spark a curiosity around what knit, as a material and a system of making, could be in the future.

I am always working on multiple and varied projects. I use biomimicry as a methodology to inform my design practice, so at an early stage in a project I might be reading scientific papers or talking to experts about their research. This helps me to think about the process of knit design in unconventional ways. At the University of Leeds, we are fortunate to have power knitting machines, and I spend considerable time programming and testing. As an academic, it is important for me to publish my research, through written publications in books and journals, and via exhibition work and presentations.

My skill set combines expert technical knowledge of knit structures and materials with a unique creative-design perspective

Fig. 8.18 Practice-based academic researchers, such as Dr Jane Scott, showcase their work both in publications and through exhibitions. The Royal Armouries Museum provided an impressive setting for this large-scale installation of Jane's architectural textiles.

and the knowledge of specialist programming systems and machine technologies. I think that opportunities in the future will become increasingly interdisciplinary. It is therefore critical to have a deep understanding of knitting, yarns and fibres, and the ability to work collaboratively, so that shared knowledge can lead to greater understanding.

ABOUT THE AUTHORS

Cathy Challender has been teaching knitwear design for over twenty-five years and has a passion for hunting through knitting archives in the hope to learn new things from old stuff. After graduating from the Royal College of Art in 1989, she worked as a knitwear designer in London. Cathy has been a trustee and supporter of Ruddington Framework Knitters' Museum for many years and belongs to the Worshipful Company of Framework Knitters.

Kandy Diamond is an artist and designer whose creations blur the lines between product and art. Her brand Knit and Destroy has seen international success; a book, *Knit and Destroy … Gets Handy!*, featuring hand-knitting versions of her designs, was published in 2013. Her work aims to challenge cultural preconceptions, by offering an alternative representation of knitting and creating pieces that are at odds with the embedded stereotype.

Helen Hill has extensive knowledge of fashion knitwear design in both the education sector and the industry sector. Her industry experience was gained within manufacturing and supplier businesses, where she established her expertise in knitwear design development, garment construction and mass-production manufacturing. Helen also has a strong research interest in sustainable clothing.

Will Hurley specializes in computer-aided design (CAD)/computer-aided manufacturing (CAM) technology for the production of knitwear and knitted textiles. This ranges from basic knitting and CAD principles to complex, creative knitting techniques. His research into the novel application of knitted structures and the integration of electrically active and passive materials has led to the development of three-dimensional knitted shoes, electrically heated gloves, knitted sensors, switches and three-dimensional burns garments.

Ian McInnes, Principal Lecturer in Fashion Knitwear Design and Knitted Textiles, has worked successfully as a knitwear and knitted-textile designer in Milan, London and Scotland. He is sought by prestigious academic institutions as an academic advisor and external examiner in the UK and internationally. Ian has worked on the Scottish Academy of Fashion project and co-curated the Knitting Nottingham exhibition held in 2014. His research focus is drawing for knitted-textile innovation.

Claire Preskey worked as a knitted-swatch designer for fourteen years, selling original trend-forward knitted-fashion-fabric designs across both commercial and designer market levels. Her main clients included Donna Karan, TSE Cashmere, Paul & Joe, Marks & Spencer and Banana Republic. More recently, Claire has exhibited fabrics at SpinExpo Shanghai and had creative knitted-fabric direction published on WGSN.

Juliana Sissons moved into knitwear design after training in Savile Row tailoring, pattern cutting and costume design. Her clients have included Alexander McQueen, Louis Vuitton, Shelley Fox, Joe Casely-Hayford, Koji Tatsuno, the BBC and the Victoria and Albert Museum. Juliana has written the first and second editions of the *Knitwear* volume that is part of the collection of Basic Fashion Design books (AVA Academia/Bloomsbury).

Jane Thomson has over twenty-five years of experience in knitwear design and fabric development for the fashion, interior and hosiery markets. A co-founder of the contemporary design company Acorn Conceptual Textiles, Jane has collaborated with clients including Louis Vuitton, Calvin Klein, Ralph Lauren and Abercrombie & Fitch. A practising fine artist, Jane teaches fashion illustration and design generation for UK undergraduate courses.

Amy Twigger Holroyd is a designer, maker, lecturer and researcher. She ran her craft fashion knitwear label, Keep & Share, for ten years; her Reknit Revolution project promotes the reworking of existing knitted items using knitting-based skills, techniques and knowledge. Amy completed her PhD at Birmingham Institute of Art and Design in 2013, and her book *Folk Fashion: Understanding Homemade Clothes* (I.B.Tauris) was published in 2017.

ACKNOWLEDGEMENTS

We would like to thank all those who have supported us in the development of this book. We are grateful to all of the student and graduate designers who have allowed us to feature their development work and final designs, and the industry, research, museum and archive contacts who have generously given permission for use of their images. We would especially like to thank graphic designer Alice Stone and photographer Rasha Kotaiche for their work, which forms such an important component of this book. We are also indebted to the industry professionals who contributed such thoughtful accounts for the case studies in Chapter 8.

More generally, we thank all of our BA and MA students for their creativity and passion for fashion knitwear design, which helps us, as teaching staff, to keep learning about our discipline. We are grateful to Nottingham Trent University and our colleagues in the Fashion, Textiles and Knitwear department and the marketing team for their support. We particularly thank Helen Merrin and Heather Parsonage for their invaluable advice. Final thanks must go to our families for their patience and encouragement as we developed and finalized the manuscript alongside the demands of a busy academic calendar.

WEBSITES AND FURTHER READING

Fashion and knitwear design

Black, S., *Knitwear in Fashion* (Thames & Hudson, 2005)

Brown, C., *Knitwear Design* (Laurence King Publishing, 2013)

Davies, H., *Fashion Designers' Sketchbooks* (Laurence King Publishing, 2010)

Dawber, M., *The Complete Fashion Sketchbook* (Batsford, 2013)

Dieffenbacher, F., *Fashion Thinking* (AVA Publishing, 2013)

Fletcher, K., *Sustainable Fashion and Textiles*, 2nd edition (Routledge, 2014)

Fletcher, K., *Craft of Use: Post-Growth Fashion* (Routledge, 2016)

Rissanen, T. and McQuillan, H., *Zero Waste Fashion Design*, (Bloomsbury Publishing Plc, 2015)

Sissons, J., *Knitwear: An Introduction to Contemporary Design*, 2nd edition (Bloomsbury Publishing Plc, 2018)

Trend forecasting, trade fairs and industry news

Drapers: https://www.drapersonline.com

Pitti Immagine Filati (Florence): https://www.pittimmagine.com

Première Vision (Paris, New York): http://www.premierevision.com/en/

SpinExpo (Shanghai, Paris, New York): http://www.spinexpo.com

WGSN: http://www.wgsn.com/en/

Fibres

The Better Cotton Initiative: https://bettercotton.org

The British Alpaca Society: http://www.bas-uk.com

The Campaign for Wool: http://www.campaignforwool.org

The Woolmark Company: https://www.woolmark.com

Yarn sourcing

Fairfield Yarns: http://www.fairfieldyarns.co.uk

Knit Works London: http://knitworkslondon.com/yarn-store

Uppingham Yarns: https://www.wools.co.uk

Yeoman Yarns: https://yeoman-yarns.co.uk

Manufacturing

British Standards Institute: https://www.bsigroup.com/
en-GB/
Fashion Revolution: https://www.fashionrevolution.org
UK Fashion & Textile Association (care labelling): http://
www.care-labelling.co.uk

Repair

Love Your Clothes: https://www.loveyourclothes.org.uk
Reknit Revolution: https://reknitrevolution.org

Knitting history

Books

Farrell, J., *Socks and Stockings* (Batsford, 1992)
Felkin, W., *A History of the Machine-Wrought Hosiery and Lace Manufactures* (David & Charles, [1867] 1967)
Gulvin, C., *The Scottish Hosiery and Knitwear Industry: 1680–1980* (John Donald Publishers Limited, 1984)
Mason, S.A., *The History of the Worshipful Company of Framework Knitters* (Worshipful Company of Framework Knitters, 2000)
Millington, J.T. and Chapman S.D. (eds), *Four Centuries of Machine Knitting* (Knitting International, 1989)
Palmer, M., *Framework Knitting* (Shire Publications, 2002)
Rutt, R., *A History of Hand Knitting* (Batsford, 1987)

Websites

In The Loop at Winchester School of Art (Knitting Reference Library, Knitting Collections and In The Loop conference series): https://www.southampton.ac.uk/intheloop
Knitting & Crochet Guild: http://kcguild.org.uk
Knitting Together: The Heritage of the East Midlands Knitting Industry: http://knittingtogether.org.uk
Ruddington Framework Knitters' Museum: https://www.frameworkknittersmuseum.org.uk
Shetland Textile Museum: https://www.shetlandtextilemuseum.com
Sir Richard Arkwright's Cromford Mills: https://www.cromfordmills.org.uk
Strutt's North Mill Museum: http://belpernorthmill.org
Victoria and Albert Museum Knitting Collection: https://www.vam.ac.uk/collections/knitting
Wigston Framework Knitters' Museum: http://wigstonframeworkknitters.org.uk

Index